P9-CFJ-760

PREACHING FOR TODAY

Clyde E. Fant

———

PREACHING

FOR

TODAY

———

HARPER & ROW, PUBLISHERS
New York, Hagerstown, San Francisco, London

PREACHING FOR TODAY. Copyright © 1975 by Clyde E. Fant. All rights reserved. Printed in the United States of America. No part of this book may be used or reproduced in any manner whatsoever without written permission except in the case of brief quotations embodied in critical articles and reviews. For information address Harper & Row, Publishers, Inc., 10 East 53rd Street, New York, N.Y. 10022. Published simultaneously in Canada by Fitzhenry & Whiteside Limited, Toronto.

First HARPER & ROW PAPERBACK edition published in 1977.

Designed by C. Linda Dingler

Library of Congress Cataloging in Publication Data

Fant, Clyde E
   Preaching for today.
   Includes bibliographical references.
   1. Preaching. I. Title.
BV4211.2.F36 1975   251   74-4640
ISBN 0-06-062332-2

77 78 79 10 9 8 7 6 5 4 3 2 1

To my father

CONTENTS

PREFACE

Nothing is more sought today by laymen and preachers alike than a meaningful sound from the pulpit. They both know, even if they cannot say it, that the Word is neither thunder nor angel speech. What it is, or what it should be, however, is another matter. This book is about that. It is an attempt to unify the practice of preaching, from sermon construction to pulpit delivery, within a meaningful theology of proclamation.

Most books about preaching are written by specialists in one preaching field or the other—history of preaching, theology of proclamation, communication theory, innovative sermon form, sermon delivery, and so on—and those are the books that do me the most good. The thoroughness and depth with which they explore each of these areas enriches me and provokes me to further study.

Sometimes I do get the feeling, however, that preaching is a bit the victim of atomization or fragmentation. And I also get that impression from pastors and specialists in other theological areas whose picture of what preaching is about is at least partial, if not distorted.

That's certainly no one's fault in particular. But it has given preaching some problems, particularly in the division between the theoretical aspects of theology of proclamation and the practical necessity of sermon construction and delivery. We clearly do not need more generalization, but it seems to me that a certain integration of these things on a common theological basis would help the wholeness of preaching.

The divorce between theology and practical homiletics is a primary reason for the parish minister's ongoing frustrations with preaching. Divorce may not be quite the proper term, however, since for many people theology and homiletics have never been wed. For some, they have never even been introduced. For all the prominence accorded the *theory* of preaching by theology, the *practice* of preaching has not enjoyed equal attention. The *what* of preaching is frequently regarded as concern enough; the *how* of preaching is merely a matter of rhetoric: "The renewal of our proclamation means that there remains only a question of what we proclaim, not the question of how we proclaim it."[1]

There are two reasons for this. First, homiletics is frequently regarded as a branch of rhetoric rather than of theology; and second, some theologians do not believe that preaching can be taught at all—which really means that the *what* of preaching can be taught, but the *how* of preaching cannot.

An example of this first point of view is to be found in Gustaf Wingren's book, *The Living Word*, an excellent inquiry into "the essential theological nature of preaching."[2] Wingren asserts, however, that "such very practical questions as the construction of the sermon, its delivery and such like obviously do not fall within our field. Homiletics as a part of practical theology has its own specific problems *which are not theological in nature*"[3] (italics mine). In other words, homiletics is indeed a division of practical theology, but the practical questions of preaching, such as the construction of the sermon and its delivery, *are not theological in nature.*

Joseph Sittler presents the second point of view, that preaching cannot be taught, when he writes, "The expectation must not be cherished, that, save for modest and obvious instruction about voice, pace, organization, and such matters preaching as a lively art of the church can be taught at all. And therefore, seminary provisions for instruction in preaching, when these exist as separate curriculum items, should be examined."[4] On the other hand, he insists that "preaching is organic to the entire actuality of the preacher,"[5] and his provocative study of preaching gives strong support to the role of preaching in the church.

How shall we evaluate these arguments? Sittler is undoubtedly right when he says, "Disciplines correlative to preaching can be taught, but preaching as an act of witness cannot be taught."[6] It is also true that practical homiletics has been fragmented away from the whole of the theological enterprise as a separate discipline. But this is the very point I am making: The fragmentation of preaching is only made worse when the subject is either left in theological abstraction or relegated to "modest and obvious instruction about voice, pace, organization, and such matters."

Of course preaching cannot be taught—but then, can theology? Technically, it cannot. Obviously systematic theology wishes to teach its students to "do theology," not merely to convey conclusions to them about theology, or to teach them the history of theology, or even to suggest to them helpful methodology for arriving at theological conclusions. At that point we are all equally helpless; we cannot teach a student to be a Barth or a Brunner in the theological study any more than we can teach him to be a Barth or a Brunner in the pulpit. All teaching shares this problem. Even if a musician could teach his student *how* Bach did what he did, he still couldn't teach him to *do* what Bach did.

But is this not all beside the point? If theology does not unite the human dilemma with its ultimate concerns, is it truly theology? Likewise, if preaching has no theological basis for its considerations of form, method, and delivery, can it be justified as a practice at all?

We must remember that "preaching is preaching only when a sermon is being preached. No systematic consideration of preaching can afford to pass over this simple fact!" as Rudolf Bohren puts it. He adds, "Particular attention should be paid to the practical aspect of preaching. The act of preaching is a particularly important subject for systematic theology."[7] The practical aspects of speaking the sermon *must be united theologically* with the theoretical aspects of preaching.

If we do not do so, then preaching as a practical act within the church will be hopelessly schizoid. One-half of its personality will be Hebrew-Christian, and the other half will be Greek-pagan. Perhaps the theoretical idea of preaching, or even the

content of the sermon itself, may be solidly theological and
Christian; but the *actual* sermon, the *preached* sermon, which
cannot avoid its essential entanglement with questions of form,
methodology, and delivery, will be weakly rhetorical and
pagan. We will have "severed the head of preaching from
theology and dropped it into the basket of rhetoric held by
Aristotle."[8]

What is to be done in this case? Shall the Jew marry the Greek,
and the Jew live tenuously, if not happily, ever after? Shall
Judeo-Christian proclamation cohabit with Greco-pagan
rhetoric? If so, it will never be more than a marriage of con-
venience, for the twain shall never become one flesh. There has
never been, and there will never be, more than one possible
result from this uneasy union. Preaching will go on being
praised in theory and damned in practice.

But there is no need for this impossible situation. Theology
itself provides us with the decisive clue. The divine-human
nature of its concerns are precisely those of preaching: "The
Word became flesh and dwelt among us (John 1:14, RSV)."
*Form, methodology, and delivery are nothing more, and
nothing less, than the word of God taking on flesh and dwelling
among us.*

These practical questions are indeed the painful embarrassment of preaching, but no more so than the human form of Jesus
of Nazareth was a stumbling block to the Jews and a joke to the
Greeks. Any attempt on the part of theology, no matter how well
intentioned, to sever these "human" questions from the
"divine" nature of Christian proclamation can only be viewed
as another error of abstract, speculative theology which would
force preaching to live in a house it has just torn down for
itself.

Freeing the pure soul of Christian proclamation—its content
—from the wicked body of actual pulpit practice—its presentation—will not do. The salvation of preaching can only be the
salvation of a living body, not an abstract soul. Then, and only
then, can preaching at last be made whole.

I certainly do not believe that this book accomplishes such a large task. But I do think it is worth a try, and I hope that others will do more ably that which I believe I have realized to be worthwhile. As C. S. Lewis once put it, that part of the line where I thought I could serve best also seemed to be thinnest, and so to it I naturally went.

Perhaps one additional word of explanation is necessary. Throughout this work I have used the term *incarnational preaching*. I believe the context will suggest, if not completely define, what I do and do not mean by it. But by no means do I intend to suggest a confusion between the unique event in Christ and what happens in preaching. I do believe, however, that the incarnation is the truest theological model for the mysterious divine-human preaching event, which is neither all of man nor all of God, but which partakes of both with precisely the same degree of mystery and humility as that reality in Jesus of Nazareth.

It is always impossible to give adequate thanks to the many people who contribute to the writing of a work such as this. I have dedicated this book to the memory of my father, who died during the writing of it. More than anyone I have ever known— and I am not alone in this opinion—he knew better than anyone how to communicate with people. His twenty-five years of honorable public service proved that. And longer yet, he spoke in churches and taught the Bible to men in his own church. I am sure no one will object if I express my gratitude first for his life-long contribution to this book—and me. Not only in speaking, but in understanding people, he was my first and greatest teacher.

I am also grateful to my classes and graduate seminars for their contribution to this work. They suggested many ideas in the years that these concepts were being discussed with them, and they have offered good advice as they listened to the final copy read—even if I did get unmerciful kidding for reading a manu-script!

As usual, I would have been absolutely helpless if Mrs. Kara Hammer had been just a typist for the book instead of the com-pletely able and gracious project secretary which she is. I

suspect that most of us who write would never do very much if
it were not for the generous contribution of persons like herself.
Linda McKay and Caren Sue Jones also worked hard to decipher
unreadable notes and find all of those things I am always mis-
placing.

Discussions with friends helped in more ways than one—the
spirit needs community as well as the mind. I hesitate even to
start such a list, but I cannot fail to express appreciation to Don
Hammer, Cecil White, Bill Pinson, Douglas Ezell, Virtus Gideon,
Ray Vickrey, Glen Edwards, Don Dilday, David Matthews,
Gerald Marsh, Dan Day, Jack Coldiron, Farrar Patterson, Lacoste
Munn, and Milton Ferguson, each of whom contributed in his
own unique way. I am especially grateful for the support and
encouragement of the Foundation for Christian Communication
in general and of Vester Hughes, Dr. James Harris, and Vann
Pratt in particular.

Finally, I must again thank my wife and family for all their
help and patience—they needed it!

PREACHING FOR TODAY

1

THE STUBBORN PULPIT

Whatever virtues the pulpit may lack, stubbornness is not one of them. The vine over Jonah's head would have withered in less than a day if it had suffered the heated blasts directed at the pulpit across the centuries. But for the most part, the preacher goes on sitting in the shade of his sermonic vines, not sure if they are merely gnawed of worms or cursed of God—or both— even if they no longer flourish as they once did, and even if the sultry east winds of criticism sometimes make him want to curse God and die.

No part of the worship of the church has been so generously and ecumenically roasted as preaching, but likewise no aspect of its worship has been so generally and ecumenically practiced. In fact, the act of preaching may be the most truly ecumenical observance of the church. It has a longer continuous history of virtually unanimous practice among all groups, Protestant and Catholic, than any other element in her worship. Baptism and the Lord's Supper are as generally observed, but the meaning and method of observance of these rites vary widely from group to group. Enter any place of worship on any Sunday, however, and, like it or not, you probably can count on hearing a sermon not very different from the one you heard anywhere else the Sunday before.

Preaching, then, has a double stubbornness: it is stubbornly the same, and it is stubbornly there.

Whether this is good or bad depends on one's point of view. Legions of critics from the first century on have not liked it one bit. Despite the hoary history of pulpit bombardment, every generation of preachers seems to get caught by surprise in the attack. Previously this awareness crept up on most preachers about the age of pulpit puberty—which is an indeterminable age somewhere between pulpit innocence and pulpit senility—although some men never seem to go through it at all.

If there is anything at all different, however, about the attacks on preaching in the last half of the twentieth century, it is the around-the-clock nature of the bombing and the early serious-ness with which young ministers are regarding this criticism. It is hard to evaluate the self-doubt of previous generations; so we will never know how badly other generations of preachers were unnerved by the shelling of the pulpit. But it obviously hasn't done much to encourage preaching in this century, as mani-fested by the widespread skepticism of the pulpit ministry and the decidedly apologetic tone of those writings which seek to defend preaching in the parish ministry.

If abundance of criticism is any criterion, however, no gener-ation of preachers has ever had much ease in Zion.

As a matter of fact, "to a large extent, the pulpit has from the first century received poor reviews (2 Cor. 10:9–10)."[1] Perhaps Selden overstated the case in his *Table Talk* when he asserted that "preaching in the first sense of the word ceased as soon as ever the gospel was written," but at least he proves that criti-cism wasn't long in beginning.[2] Brilioth quotes criticisms of various preachers and their preaching from the second century onward, including Tertullian's critique of Melito of Sardis and Porphyry's accusations against Origen.[3] In the fourth century preaching was said to have degenerated into a tool for eccle-siastical and political deceit.[4] The preachers of the seventh century were accused of "having too great a tendency to moral-ize, to allow every text in the Bible to become the starting point for an ethical admonition which was primarily intended to emphasize the church's precepts on penance, fasting, and good works."[5]

During the Middle Ages the sermon was attacked as mechanical, dull, and usually nothing more than a poor plagiarism of earlier works.[6] In the sixteenth century preaching was the butt of ridicule by the laity who found it to be incredibly boring and who passed the time away by sleeping, chattering, or playing simple games. Sometimes, if provoked, they even attacked the sermon during the service itself. One woman who had been rebuked in the midst of a sermon for gossiping with her neighbor promptly jumped up and said angrily, "Indeed sir, I know the one who has been doing the most babbling! For I do but whisper a word with my neighbor, and thou hast babbled there all this hour."[7] The sermons of this entire period were "no more than the dry bones of a decaying art."[8]

The preaching of the seventeenth century was criticized as one-sided and full of exaggeration.[9] In England, Robert South ridiculed the ignorance of the preachers of that age, saying that "to be blind was with them the proper qualification of a spiritual guide; and to be book-learned as they call it, and to be irreligious were almost synonymous terms."[10] For some years after 1660 the name of Charles I was more used in sermons than that of Christ. In 1670 John Eachard complained bitterly in his tract, "The Grounds and Contempt of the Clergy Inquired Into," about the unintelligible, unnatural, and uncommunicative speech of the pulpit. In The Reformed Pastor, Richard Baxter devoted twenty-four closely printed pages to a survey of the sins of "ministers of the Gospel from the days of Christ until now."[11]

In 1761 John Harman wrote a scathing critique of preaching, The Crooked Disciple's Remarks Upon the Blind Guides' Method of Preaching. In 1799 Eli Forbes published The Inoffensive Ministry Described, which claimed that preaching had degenerated to a level far below that of previous years. One critic labeled the preaching of that age "dull, duller, dullest," and John Caird declared that "the pattern sermon of the Georgian era seems to have been constructed almost expressly to steer clear of all possible ways of getting human beings to listen to it."[12]

By now we might well wonder how long this cheery note continued. When *were* the "good old days" for preaching? Surely the nineteenth century was the Golden Age of Preaching! That era when sermons were the rage, and preaching was in its prime. Or was it?

A Golden Age of Preaching?

One reason for the perpetual trauma of pulpit puberty, or coming of age in the pulpit, is the incredibly persistent myth of the "Golden Age of Preaching," whenever that was. Ask any generation of preachers, and it was exactly three generations earlier. And that holds true all the way back, at least to within three generations of the apostolic age. (The apostles themselves were not troubled by such delusions—they just wanted to return to the Golden Age of Rabbinicism.)

The net result of this absolute figment of imagination is the feeling on the part of every preacher that he is among the first generation of preachers to be chained to the rock of the pulpit and have his liver torn out by the giant birds of criticism, only to have it grow back before the next Sunday. This preaching Prometheus resents his punishment for attempting to bring fire from the gods to men, and he is sure that in the Golden Age of the ancients things were different.

This mythical era is usually located in the nineteenth century. Wasn't that the century of the "pulpit-princes"? Weren't Spurgeon, Robertson, Beecher, Brooks, Maclaren, Liddon, Dale, Broadus, Parker, Talmage, Newman, Whyte, and Bushnell the glory of the pulpit? Wasn't "sermon-tasting" the Sunday rage, and the morning's sermon the subject of the afternoon's conversation? Didn't tours regularly stop at the churches of the famous pastors so that tourists could hear them? Was there ever such a time for preaching?

Nevertheless, the preachers who stood with both feet in the middle of that century did not see it as any "Golden Age," but just as another tough, demanding time to be a preacher.

F. W. Robertson, probably the most widely used homiletical

example from that century, saw his age as a time of declining
influence for the pulpit: "By the change of the times the pulpit
has lost its place. It only does part of that whole which used to
be done by it alone. Once it was newspaper, schoolmaster,
theological treatise, a stimulant to good works, historical lecture, metaphysics, etc., all in one. Now these are proportioned
out to different officers, and the pulpit is no more the pulpit of
three centuries back."[13] In a letter to a friend he wrote, "I wish I
did not hate preaching so much, but the degradation of being a
Brighton preacher is almost intolerable."[14]

Despondent, moody Robertson was not the only man of his
time to mourn the passing of the pulpit. In 1882, when Mahaffy
wrote "The Decay of Modern Preaching," Spurgeon, Liddon,
Parker, Beecher, Maclaren, and Brooks were at the height of
their careers. And in 1923 Joseph Fort Newton quoted the
London *Times* as saying that, "For the present at least, the
noble art of the pulpit must be considered as lost," and asking,
"If the great sermons . . . of Bishop Butler were preached today,
would they fill the smallest church in London?" Yet Newton
reminds us that "in his own day the Bishop sat in his castle
brooding over the decay of religion, while the miners, touched
by the wondrous evangelism of Wesley, were singing hymns of
praise almost under his window."[15]

If any further evidence is needed, a partial list of critical
articles from the nineteenth century should be convincing:

1805, "Defects of Preaching" (London, *Christian Observer* 4:462–64)
1809, "On the Assumed Popularity of Evangelical Preaching" (London, *Christian Observer* 10:484–92, 627–28)
1811, "On the Little Success which Attends the Preaching of the
Gospel" (London, *Christian Observer* 10:746–49)
1868, "Bad Preaching" (London, *Broadway* 1:439 ff.)
1868, Caird, John. "The Declining Influence of the Pulpit in Modern
Times" (London, *Good Works* 9:193–200)
1876, "Dull Sermons," Charles H. Grundy (London, *Macmillan's
Magazine* 34:264–67)
1877, Brown, James Baldwin. "Is the Pulpit Losing Its Power?" (Boston, *Living Age* 133:304–13)
1878, "Is the Modern Pulpit a Failure?" (last chapter in *Lectures on*

Preaching by Matthew Simpson: "It has become fashionable in certain circles to speak of the failure of the pulpit." He calls this an "old song.")

1896, Haweis, Hugh Reginald. *The Dead Pulpit* (London)

1899, Stephen J. Herben. "Is the Power of the Pulpit Waning?" (New York, 1899 *Methodist Review* 59:896—910)

And note this one:

1899, "The Pulpit in the Good Old Days," Walter Slater (London: *Temple Bar* 85:557—59)

No age seems so golden as in the afterglow of its sunset. The nineteenth was indeed a strong century for preaching, but *no stronger than the twentieth*. Every teacher of preaching is pressed to answer the question, "Where are the great preachers today?" The answer is, "Right where they always have been— few and far between."

At the most, no one could produce more than fifteen to twenty truly memorable names from the nineteenth century of preaching. That is a fine number, actually, but nearly that many could be produced from the twentieth century—and it still has a quarter of its life remaining. (Skeptical? How about Harry Emerson Fosdick, Dick Sheppard, William Temple, Studdert Kennedy, Karl Barth, Ronald Knox, Emil Brunner, George Buttrick, Paul Scherer, Reinhold Niebuhr, Samuel Shoemaker, Leslie Weatherhead, Fulton Sheen, James Stewart, William Sangster, D. T. Niles, Billy Graham, Helmut Thielicke, Martin Luther King, Martyn Lloyd-Jones. Don't agree with all of them? Did you with all of the nineteenth-century preachers?)

Already the first half of the twentieth century is being fondly remembered, and the last half is being anticipated with the same morose depression which is the inevitable insecurity of the pulpit.

None of this should be understood as saying that all centuries are alike in the quality of their preaching or in the reception accorded to it. That is obviously untrue. Some ages have been bleak and others have been better. But it does say that every generation of preachers tends to romanticize the heroic past and to be overly pessimistic about the present.

This short-sightedness produces a kind of cave-mentality for the ministry. The darkest view is always ahead, and the brightest light comes from behind us, from where we entered. We do not need to dispute the very real problems which preaching has today. But we do need to lay to rest once and for all the unrealistic "Golden Age" myth, and we do need to know that pulpit criticism was not born in our generation.

Recent Criticism

This doesn't mean that we haven't had our share of it. Whatever preaching's problems in the twentieth century, at least it hasn't had any false delusions about itself as an age of preaching, golden or otherwise.

At the "turn of the century" (about as close to the popular idea of the Good Old Days as you can get), the Good Old Articles on preaching carried such encouraging titles as "The Decadence of Preaching" (1903);[16] "Is the Pulpit a Coward's Castle?" (1905);[17] "Why Sermons Make Us Go to Sleep" (1908);[18] "Is Preaching Obsolete?" (1911);[19] and the question most of the preachers must have been asking, "What Is to Become of the Preacher?" (1911).[20]

The two decades which followed sharpened the attack: "Is Preaching Futile?" (1920);[21] "Why the Pew Is Listless" (1924);[22] "The Decline of Preaching" (1925)[23] (by now it should be apparent that preaching must be descending the world's longest hill—wherever and whenever its peak was); "The Futility of Sermons" (1925);[24] Fosdick's famous article, "What Is the Matter with Preaching?" (1928);[25] "Can the Protestant Sermon Survive?" (1932);[26] and the blunt question, "A Halt to Preaching?" (1936).[27]

More recent criticism of preaching has been characterized by increased perceptivity and articulateness. Some of it has continued to be marked by an unawareness of history and a desire to work out all of the problems of the church on preaching, but much of it has hit preaching where it hurts, or ought to hurt. What are the sore spots for the critics?

Almost everything. Joseph Sittler says, "Preaching is in trouble everywhere."[28] A partial list of the abundant complaints against it makes that perfectly clear. Clyde Reid lists seven categories of current criticisms of preaching: (1) preachers tend to use complex, archaic language which the average person does not understand; (2) most sermons today are dull, boring, and uninteresting; (3) most preaching today is irrelevant; (4) preaching today is not courageous preaching; (5) preaching does not communicate; (6) preaching does not lead to change in persons; (7) preaching has been overemphasized.[29]

Reuel Howe lists six complaints by laymen concerning preaching: (1) sermons often contain too many complex ideas; (2) sermons have too much analysis and too little answer; (3) sermons are too formal and too impersonal; (4) sermons use too much theological jargon; (5) sermons are too propositional; not enough illustrations; (6) too many sermons simply reach a dead end and give no guidance to commitment and action.[30]

Others involved in counseling are quoted by Gene Bartlett as raising these criticisms from their experience: (1) preaching clearly seems directive; (2) all preaching generalizes (!); (3) much preaching is guilt producing; (4) sermon-listening may divert the listener away from his real problems; (5) the public preacher may violate his role as private listener.[31]

Besides these complaints, a summary list could be compiled from the many other writers who have criticized preaching:

1. The *influence* of the sermon has been generally challenged. Does it *affect* anything? Does it change anything? Is it important enough to claim as much of the minister's time as it demands? Is it, in fact, a valid part of the Christian task? Berton,[32] Berger,[33] Glock and Stark,[34] Dittes,[35] and others raise these questions.

2. The *form* of the sermon has been questioned. In its present form, can the sermon communicate? In addition to Reid, this question is also raised by Howe who says that younger preachers are challenging the usefulness of traditional monological preaching.[36] New alternatives, notably utilization of small

groups, are called for in various forms by Berton,[37] Symanowski,[38] Wenzel,[39] and Wedel.[40]

3. The *content* of the sermon has been sharply criticized. Harvey Cox says that preaching is weak because it does not "confront people with the new reality which has occurred and because the summons is issued in general rather than specific terms"; and he adds, "We have departed today from the preaching of the Apostles."[41] Doberstein,[42] Jensen,[43] and Ebeling,[44] among others, emphasize that it is not preaching, but the weak content of *our* preaching which is at fault.

4. The *preacher* of the sermon has also come in for a considerable share of the criticism. In fact, increasingly the "declining" influence of preaching, the irrelevance of its content, and the problems with its form are being laid at the personal doorstep of the preacher himself. Helmut Thielicke has particularly located his criticism at that point.[45]

In short, every aspect of preaching is under attack today just as it always has been from the beginning. Our review has made it abundantly plain that no age of pulpit proclamation has ever escaped heavy criticism.

This evidence should have two effects on today's preacher: first, *sobering*, when he realizes how stubbornly unwilling or unable preaching has been to profit from its mistakes; and second, *reassuring*, when he realizes that the first sound of criticism is not the last note of hope for the future of preaching. He needs this balanced perspective to keep him from either unbounded optimism or unwarranted despair.

Nevertheless, although sharp criticism does not in itself signal the end of preaching, that is no excuse for continually ignoring it or not seeking to eliminate its causes. Preaching has stubbornly refused to acknowledge the validity of the charges against it and to repent, to change for the better, to be what it claims; and having failed to satisfy its critics with its life, it is now being invited to do so with its death.

Outside of obligingly stretching out prone, what else can preaching do to remedy its problems? It seems to me that we need an adequate perspective on the development of these problems if we are to deal with them seriously.

The Preaching Cycle

The first step in this direction has already been taken. That is, becoming aware of the long history of pulpit criticism and realizing that we have not desecrated Eden, that we have not been driven out of the Golden Age of preaching by our sins, and that no angel with a flaming sword bars our return to a preaching paradise.

When Joseph Sittler says, "Preaching is in trouble everywhere," he goes on to add, "Of course preaching is in trouble. Whence did we ever manufacture the assumption that it was ever to be in anything but trouble?"[46] It is only our duty, as we shall see, to make sure it is in trouble for the right reasons.

The second step is to understand that preaching, like the church whose servant it is, participates in a definite cycle. At times, preaching has enjoyed great prominence in the church; at other times, it has been less than nothing. But when preaching becomes everything in the church, it quickly becomes nothing for the next generation. There is but one God, and he will tolerate no other. The foolish idolizing of the pulpit and the fatuous worshiping of the cult of personality inevitably lead to the decline of preaching.

Nothing is surer than this. Only when the pulpit is servant is it given a place at the table; when it ceases to be the servant of the Word and fights for the chief seats, it is told to "go down there and sit." But when it becomes the servant of all, as in the parable, preaching finds its true greatness.

With respect to the proclamation of the gospel, a definite cycle can be observed for two thousand years: *search, discovery, excitement, routinization, boredom, disillusionment, search.* Naturally this order is not mechanically reproduced in every generation, but the broad outlines are plainly discernible in Christian history. Furthermore, there are smaller waves of this effect going on within the larger cycle. The church as a whole might be at one point, while individual locales might be at an altogether different stage of development.

Since this is a cycle, we might begin at any point in examining it. But *search* will do as a starting point. Preaching always begins in a search for an adequate means of conveying the Word. Since the gospel is good news, the Word is always in search of words to publish glad tidings; the church struggles to find expression for the faith once delivered in the midst of a living contemporary community.

This search, born of faith in the Word, leads to *discovery;* discovery of words for the realities it has grasped, however imperfectly, and of means for expressing these words to its age. New forms and methods of preaching are born.

Great *excitement* attends this discovery—which usually is made initially by a few—as others seize upon the words and means which have been found faithful servants of the Word.

A process of *routinization* follows, wherein that which was spontaneously done in its beginnings is made the common practice and eventually the official program for proclaiming the faith. Deviations in content, language, and even style are frowned upon as unorthodox, if not rejected outright or surpressed.

Boredom quickly sets in as the church suffers from the deadening routine of "the right way to do it." During this period the church frequently searches its memory to recall "how it was done" when its preaching was successful; and anyone who asks painful questions of the cultically correct method is quickly reminded that these approved practices are identically the same as those which produced the Golden Days, now receding rapidly into myth.

Disillusionment follows, as more and more of the faithful discover that the standard routine does not work any longer, that the words and means that were once strong and honest servants have now become tottering and powerless tyrants. These old systems are quickly deposed, but only cynicism inherits their empty thrones. For awhile cynicism and nihilism reign, and only celebrating the emptiness brings any satisfaction. Sooner or later, however, the painful reality of this hollow meaninglessness seizes the church, and it is led again into the agonizing *search* for authentic words.

This search is always agonizing because the pioneers of this movement cannot resist substituting newer meaningless cultural clichés for the older cultic language they so emphatically reject. But when someone, somewhere, in this process realizes that these efforts are no more than updated versions of the same mistake that has held the Word captive all along, and waits in humility to listen until it speaks fresh words to him, then the Word becomes flesh again and discovery begins.

It would take both a prophet and his son to say where we are now in this cycle. The answer would vary anyway from group to group, and even from person to person. Collectively, however, it appears obvious that we are not at the crest of the wave, and quite likely we have emerged a bit from its trough. A good guess would be that most of us in this last half of the twentieth century are somewhere in the process of search—either quite early in that stage, or perhaps, for a few, on the edge of discovery.

It will likely be a long while before a new process of routinization emerges. We may never see a new synthesis in our lifetime; like it or not, we may spend our lives searching for the Promised Land. But prediction is really impossible.

In the face of its often failures, however, what confidence can preaching have that discovery is possible at all, that the Word can again find fresh words for its message? What hope sustains preaching? What keeps the pulpit stubbornly there?

2

THE STUBBORN HOPE

Can the stubbornness of the pulpit—not its stubbornness in resistance to change, but the stubbornness of its existence—simply be attributed to inertia, to habit, to some mysterious hold which the pulpit continues to exercise through the centuries? Or is there something more basically stubborn about the pulpit? Does preaching sustain some kind of internal relationship with the Christian faith rather than merely being a cultic, temporal expression? Could it be that preaching itself is essentially and authentically Christian?

Preaching as Authentically Christian

If we want to answer this question, we have to look at the origins of the Christian sermon. Did it arise from Hebrew soil, or is preaching nothing more than a Greek intrusion, a pagan rhetorical overlay on the Christian faith?

Amos Wilder insists that "the spoken and written word have a basic role in the Christian faith," and he sees the background for this role in the Old Testament:

The religion of Israel is very much a matter of hearing rather than of seeing. Even God's actions are spoken of by the prophets as his word. No man can see God and live, but he is known in his speaking. By contrast it is the gods of the nations that are mute, and their visible

images are dumb. As we read in Psalm 115:7, "They do not make a
sound in their throat." Throughout scripture, revelation is identified
above all with speaking and hearing . . . rather than with the imagery
of the visual arts. . . . Of course, like all religions Christianity has its
sacred actions and spectacles, sacred places and times, sacred arts and
objects, but it is in connection with God's speaking that they are
sacred. . . . Language, then, is more fundamental than graphic repre-
sentation, except where the latter is itself a transcript in some sense of
the word of God.[1]

This emphasis on the priority of *word* in the Old Testament
is apparent even in the creation narratives. In the Book of
Genesis, man is created by the word of God. All of God's
creatures are called into being, and man himself is created in
the image of God in that he also speaks, names, and communicates.[2] Likewise, in Exodus 33:11 we are told that "the Lord
used to speak to Moses face to face, as a man speaks with his
friend." And Wilder says, "The rhetorics of the Old Testament
represent the response of man to the address of God, and their
form and style are elicited by the self-communication of God."[3]

Hebrew precedence for Christian preaching is also evident in
the proclamations of the rulers of Israel as well as in the
preaching of the prophets. In Isaiah, *proclamation* is used to
describe the activity of the Servant of the Lord (Isa. 61:1). Jesus
later declared that his ministry was the fulfillment of these
prophetic words and thereby traced his ministry of proclaiming to Old Testament sources (Luke 4:21).[4] Brilioth agrees that
"A clear line extends from Old Testament prophecy to the
sermon in the Church."[5]

More directly, Christian preaching bears striking resem-
blance to the expositions of Scripture in the synagogue, perhaps even more so than the sometimes spontaneous oracles of
the Old Testament prophets: "The origin of the Christian sermon, like nearly everything in the church services, is to be
found in the Synagogue. We know from the Bible that it was
customary to expound the lesson read in the services. In the
Jewish church this developed into a hortatory address, very
near to a modern sermon."[6]

The participation of Jesus in the worship of the synagogue at Nazareth is not only interesting as an example of the earliest Christian proclamation, but also because it is one of the very few contemporary records of a Jewish synagogue service. Three elements in that narrative are particularly instructive in showing us the relationship between Jewish synagogue worship and the contemporary sermon. The sermon of Jesus in the synagogue of Nazareth was *liturgical, exegetical,* and *prophetic;* that is, it formed a part of a worship experience and was itself a mode of worship; it started from and expounded a text of Scripture; and it was a message for the present time which made the scriptural text a living word in the contemporary situation.[7] Jesus regarded his proclamation as so closely related to the framework of the Judaism of his day that he could claim its message to be one of fulfillment (Matt. 5:17). Not only in its form, then, but also in its content, the basic message of the Christian faith had Hebrew origins.[8]

The conclusion of these studies, and others, is that preaching cannot be accused of being a "Greek intrusion." It is an authentic development from Hebrew tradition: "The Christian preacher is not the successor of the Greek orator, but of the Hebrew prophet."[9] Obviously the prevailing environment for the Christian church soon became Gentile rather than Jewish, but the primary kinship of New Testament proclamation is not with this new environment but rather with its Jewish heritage.[10]

There was, in fact, a fundamental difference between the Hebrew and Greek perception of reality: "For the Hebrew, the decisive reality of the world of experience was the *word;* for the Greek it was the *thing.* . . . We can conclude for the Hebrew the most important of his senses for the experience of truth was his hearing (as well as various kinds of feeling), but for the Greek it has to be his sight; or perhaps inversely, because the Greeks were organized in a predominantly visual way and the Hebrews in a predominantly auditory way, each peoples' conception of truth was formed in increasingly different ways."[11]

One distinctive difference between Old Testament and New

Testament concepts, however, should be noted. The Old Testament rarely uses the expression, "to preach." Menoud says that the term was not used more because the Old Testament prophets were not heralds of *good news* as were the New Testament preachers: "Their commission was to exhort the elect people to remain faithful to their God. . . . These prophets were not bringing news; they asked for a better and stricter obedience to the given law."[12] Similar terms for preaching, however, were used abundantly.

This fact bears an interesting relationship to another curiosity in the New Testament. Since the most common expression translated "to preach" in the New Testament is *kerussin,* it could be expected that the most common New Testament word for preacher would be *keryx* ("herald"). But this term only occurs three times in the New Testament (1 Tim. 2:7; 2 Tim. 1:11; 2 Pet. 2:5). All of these occurrences are obviously extremely late. Why is this so?

Apparently the term was avoided because it was widely used by the pagan Stoic preachers of that day and also because the New Testament writers wished to distinguish Christian preaching from the rather mechanical heralding of the Greeks which was principally repetition by rote, and as such thereby violated the personal dynamic inherent in Christian proclamation.[13]

Because of its Hebrew heritage, early Christian preaching was also afraid of any particular vocabulary which was thought of as sacred or pious; that is, there is no precedent in early Christian speech for what is now termed "the language of Zion." To create such a language would be to engage in idolatry.

If the Hebrew tradition feared images because they promoted idolatry, they were not less strict with their own concepts regarding words. Once any term took on a fixed or magical character for Israel, its value was forfeited: "The repertory of images used in the prophets and the old tradition of Israel— such images for Israel as the vine or vineyard, the foundling or orphan, the wife—these were not allowed to become a 'holy language' or stereotypes in the post-exilic writers. They were continually reshaped and combined with new and fresh figures and expressions. The new utterance which Jesus and his followers brought into the world similarly re-created the religious vocabulary of the Old Testament."[14]

When Jesus came forth speaking, therefore, he placed himself fully in the primal oral tradition which preceded him. This in itself bears a profound theological significance: "For one thing speaking is more direct than writing, and we would expect this in him through whom God openly staged his greatest controversy with his people. . . . Jesus was a voice not a penman, a herald not a scribe, a watchman with his call in the marketplace and the Temple, and not a cry of alarm in the wilderness like John the Baptist."[15]

There was an urgency about the word of Jesus, an immediacy, a personal note which nothing but the living voice could achieve. His ministry was consistently characterized by "teaching . . . preaching . . . healing" (Matt. 4:23). In fact, Mark omits "teaching" and alters "healing" to "casting out demons" (1:39), and Luke retains only "preaching" (4:44). Mounce says, "This suggests that preaching is the most important of the three activities."[16] Jesus himself declared that it was for this reason that he had come (Mark 1:38). He committed himself freely to speech, and in this sense the early Christians also lived on the "free bounty of God."[17]

Fuchs has observed that Jesus wrote nothing and that even Paul wrote reluctantly; he was distressed by any circumstances which prevented face to face address (Gal. 4:20), and his writing itself has direct oral style, typified by imagined dialogue, direct discourse, rhetorical questions, and exclamations.[18] In this emphasis on oral style, Paul and the other disciples followed in the footsteps of Jesus: "The apostles came preaching."[19]

Although the preaching tradition of the church is clearly Hebraic in origin, this does not mean that there was no Greek influence upon it at all, or that any such influence would render preaching invalid. Why should it? Did Egyptian influence render invalid the sacrificial system of Israel? Of course

Greek rhetoric could be abused, and was; but its strong emphasis on the hearer and the plainest means of conveying a message to him were adopted by the Christian church only because this emphasis was fully in keeping with the purposes of preaching.

But it should not be overlooked that it was Greek *rhetoric* upon which the church fastened, and in so doing again asserted for itself the primacy of speech: "It is true that when the church took over the heritage of classical culture—ancient rhetoric, architecture, painting, and sculpture—it related itself to all the arts and has exploited them all ever since in changing situations. But the thesis still holds that the faith identifies fundamentally with the arts of hearing and against those of sight and touch. Even when the Christian paints, or carves, or dances, or sings he does so to a text, and identifies himself with an archetypal dialogue between God and man."[20]

From its Hebrew origins to its Greek influences in the later New Testament era, then, preaching is an insistence on the priority of word over image. Recent psychological studies corroborate the validity of this ancient viewpoint: "Reality becomes a meaningful part of consciousness only through the interpretation of real contacts by language. . . . A world without sound is a dead world: when sound is eliminated from our experience, it becomes clear how inadequate and ambiguous is the visual experience if not accompanied by auditory interpretation. . . . Vision alone without acoustic perceptions does not provide understanding."[21]

What significance does this study have for the contemporary preacher? Two implications are of particular importance.

First, preaching is authentically Christian because it represents face-to-face encounter and thereby participates in the historic medium through which God disclosed himself to man: "The word of the Lord came unto me, saying . . ." Human speech permits a degree of encounter which is profound without being idolatrous.

This leads to a second implication for preaching. The spontaneity of speech and freshness of form which Jesus employed must never be violated by crystallizing terms and forms into a "language of Zion." The tradition which commits the Christian preacher to speaking also commits him to listening. "He who aspires to the enunciation of the word must first learn to hear it; he who hears it will have found the means to articulate it."[22] When he has heard the words about him as well as the Word of God, then the preacher is ready to speak with the same freshness and freedom demanded by the preaching of the gospel in every age.

The authentically Christian nature of proclamation is a basic reason for the stubborn existence of preaching, but there is also another cause for its persistence: the importance accorded to it by theology.

Preaching as Theologically Significant

It is probably safe to say that theologians have been more enthusiastic about preaching than have preachers. The preacher would likely counter by replying that if he is frustrated with preaching, it is because he has to *do* it rather than write about it. To a certain extent, of course, he is right, and only the most obscure theologian could fail to have sympathy with him.

But one reason for the stubborn problems of the pulpit, and a major one, is the preacher's low self-esteem, both of himself in general and of his preaching task in particular. And conversely, one reason that the pulpit is still stubbornly *there* after nearly two thousand years of Christian history is the seriousness with which theologians have regarded the place of preaching in the church. In fact, at this point there is an amazing agreement among theologians, of whatever persuasion—right, left, and all points in between. Only the uniformity of the practice of preaching can rival the uniformly high place accorded to preaching in Christian theology. But I do not believe that preachers are generally aware of the striking ecumenicity among theologians at this point. How many preachers are as aware of the prominence of preaching in the theology of Bonhoeffer or Bultmann as in the theology of Barth?

If you want to present a real theological riddle, ask someone sometime what Barth, Bultmann, Ferré, Ott, Ebeling, Bonhoeffer, Niebuhr, Farmer, Tillich, Wingren, Brunner, and Gilkey have in common. If you get any answer at all (you probably won't, and you probably won't be invited back for coffee, either), it might be that they are all Christians—although a good many people wouldn't even agree on that. And if you reply to your own riddle, "They all have a high view of preaching," get ready for a dubious look followed by a vigorous argument.

But it is true, and that doesn't strike me at all as incidental. We could not think so little of what we do in the pulpit, nor could we take it so lightly, if we understood the convictions on preaching of this incredibly broad array of theologians. No one would claim that these men understand the task of preaching in the same way. They most certainly do not. But they all share a view of preaching that can only be described as high, and that in itself bears its own message.

Since theological studies do not usually pull together the ideas of these people on preaching, I think it is necessary to briefly document this claim before going on to draw conclusions from it. But anyone who really wishes to know whether it is so will have to examine the writings on preaching of these men themselves—which is precisely my reason for mentioning the subject in the first place.

It comes as no surprise to anyone that Karl Barth had a high view of preaching. In fact, he insists that if we would understand his theology we must hear all through it the question, "What is preaching?" Dip into his theology almost anywhere and you will find evidence of his regard for preaching.

For example, "Preaching is the Word of God which he himself has spoken."[23] Again, "When the gospel is preached, God speaks: there is no question of the preacher revealing anything or of a revelation being conveyed through him. . . . Our preaching does not differ in essence from that of the prophets and apostles who 'saw and touched'; the difference is due to the different historical setting in which it takes place."[24] Furthermore, "Preaching is 'God's own word.' That is to say through the activity of preaching, God himself speaks."[25] With reference to the effect of preaching Barth says, "It was pointed out above that the Church needs to be constantly renewed; it is always being created by the preaching and hearing of the Word." In this regard, for Barth "the only thing that counts is to make the Word of God heard."[26]

Barth's position is so well known that it may not come as a surprise, but it may be more difficult to believe Carl Braaten when he says, "Bultmann has always agreed with Barth at the decisive point. Both are ultimately concerned about the living Word of God as it encounters real men."[27] Or to agree that Barth and Bultmann share a "common subscription to the Later Helvetic Confession: 'Preaching the Word of God is the Word of God.'"[28]

But Bultmann is indeed unequivocal at this point: "The redemptive event is only present in the word of preaching, the word of address and claim and promise."[29] He insists that the word of preaching confronts us as the word of God. We are not to question its credentials; it is we who are questioned. We are asked whether we will believe the word or reject it. He writes, "Is not the encounter with God possible only in the fellowship where faith in God is living and preached? . . . Faith is faith in the Word of God which encounters me through the preaching of it, and preaching occurs only in the Church. . . . I should like to add: the preaching of the community enables me to participate in the eschatalogical event that has its origin in Jesus."[30] And he adds, "That means the eschatalogical occurrence continues to take place in preaching, in the address which proclaims. Preaching, therefore . . . is always the word of man and at the same time it is to be understood as God's address."[31] (At this point we should probably remind ourselves that we are quoting from Bultmann, not Barth.)

For Bultmann, preaching is also a unique kind of communication: "Christian preaching is the communication of a historical fact, so that its communication is something more than mere communication."[32] Finally, and most emphatically, "The crucified and resurrected Christ encounters us in the word of preaching, and never in any other way."[33]

When theologians as diverse as Barth and Bultmann agree so emphatically on anything, we should all take notice.

Bonhoeffer has scarcely been more often identified with preaching than Bultmann. And yet for all of his critical questions to the church and its preaching, Bonhoeffer maintained a view of Christian proclamation as high as anyone since Luther.[34] Eberhard Bethge writes: "Bonhoeffer loved to preach. When he found out that a relative of his might have a few months to live, he wrote, 'What would I do if I learned that in four to six months my life would reach the end? I believe I would still try to teach theology as I once did and to preach often.'"[35] Bethge insists that for Bonhoeffer, "discipleship, suffering, silence, worldliness—all that does not take the place of the sermon, but serves for its enthronement." His concern for the sermon "was not a matter of fearfulness," but of confidence in the ultimate value of the sermon.[36] As for his "secular interpretation of biblical concepts," Bethge says, "The secular interpretation of biblical concepts does not mean the discontinuation of preaching, but the first step toward its renewal for the world."[37]

Bonhoeffer himself wrote, "The proclaimed Word is the Incarnate Christ himself. . . . the preached Christ is the historical Christ and the present Christ. . . . He is the entrance to the historical Jesus. Therefore the proclaimed Word is not a medium of expression for something else, something which lies behind it, but it is the Christ himself walking through his congregation as the Word."[38]

Typical of the newer school of hermeneutics and its emphasis upon preaching, Gerhard Ebeling also stresses the priority of preaching: "Proclamation is the Alpha and Omega of the church's praxis."[39] Like Bonhoeffer, Ebeling identifies the purpose of theology with the function of preaching: "Theology is necessary only to the extent that it makes itself superfluous and makes proclamation necessary."[40] For Ebeling, the oral character of the Word is decisive since the Word is an "acoustical event."

Similarly Heinrich Ott says, "In so far as preaching of the gospel is a constitutive function of the Church (and there is no church without gospel proclamation; the church is essentially the sphere where the gospel is proclaimed; to declare the gospel is the church's business) gospel proclamation and theology are most closely interrelated. The coordination of theology in the church is effected through gospel proclamation."[41]

Paul Tillich has exercised considerable criticism upon the day-to-day preaching of the church. A recurring theme in his writings is the insistence that the church has not proclaimed the healing, reconciling work of the gospel with sufficient courage, selflessness, and truthfulness. Nevertheless, Tillich has a high view of the place of Christian proclamation; he "sees the value for every theology as determined for what it can do for preaching."[42] The measure of the success or failure of preaching is always the accuracy of the preacher's grasp: first, of the content of the message he has to deliver; and second, of the human situation to which he speaks.

Many other theologians are equally emphatic in stressing the place of preaching in the church. For example, *Gustaf Wingren* writes, "The task the preacher faces is that of bringing about a meeting between the Word and men. . . . The Word exists to be made known; only when it is preached is its objective content fully disclosed."[43] *P. T. Forsyth* calls preaching "the most distinctive institution in Christianity," and says "that with its preaching Christianity stands or falls."[44] *Emil Brunner* claims that wherever there is true preaching and the word of God is genuinely proclaimed, "in spite of all appearances to the contrary, the most important thing that ever happens upon this earth takes place."[45] *H. H. Farmer* says that for the church, "the prime task is to preach the gospel."[46]

Contemporary American theologians have agreed. *Martin E. Marty* writes: "The Christian cannot usually get away from verbal witness. . . . The Christian is commanded to preach. Preaching is a virtually universal activity for the churches."[47] Similarly, *Harvey Cox* reminds us that "the biblical faith, unlike Buddhism, must *speak* of God. It cannot withdraw into silence or cryptic aphorisms. A God to whom human words cannot point is not the God of the Bible."[48]

John Bright says that "the strength of the church lies in the gospel it proclaims—thus in its preaching—today, as it always has. . . . The church lives, let it be repeated, in her preaching—always has, and always will."[49] *Nels Ferré* says, "Preaching cannot take the place of the acted Word in sacrament nor the lived Word in Christian fellowship, but preaching is indispensable as the communication of the Word—the meaning and purpose of God."[50]

Likewise, *Langdon Gilkey* views the preacher as a mediator of the Word, since he believes that Christ is related to the church through the word of God as it is preached. This viewpoint has led Clyde Reid to conclude that Gilkey holds "a very high view of preaching. . . . His emphasis on the preacher as the mediator of the word would seem to place him with those who regard preaching not only as essential but as an integral part of the Christian message."[51] And *Joseph Sittler* sees preaching as integrative to the ministry of the preacher: "Preaching is not merely something a preacher does; it is a function of a preacher's whole existence concentrated at the point of declaration and interpretation."[52]

Peter Berger's shift of emphasis on preaching represents one of the most striking and potentially significant statements of recent times. In a speech to the Consultation on Church Union (COCU) meeting in Denver in 1971, Berger said, "Ages of faith are not marked by dialogue, but by proclamation," and further, "I believe a new stance is called for in our situation . . . a stance of authority." While he did not deny "the ever-new ways in which . . . [the Christian message] may be told," he asserted that "when all is said and done, the Christian community consists of those people who keep on telling this story to each other and some of whom climb up on various boxes to tell the story to others." He insisted that "if there is to be a renaissance of religion, its bearers will not be the people who have been falling all over each other to be 'relevant to modern man.' "[53]

Berger would be grossly misunderstood if his emphasis was interpreted as a call for "authoritarianism" or conservatism in theology. But just because it is not, it is all the more remarkable when he calls for authority and proclamation to cure the "demoralization and loss of nerve" of the church.

Now this in itself is noteworthy, but all the more so in light of the sweeping change of emphasis in the ten years since the publication of *The Precarious Vision*, Berger's work of 1961, in which he stated:

> But it is possible to ask even while accepting the traditional Protestant posture of the kerygma, whether an acceptance of the "world come of age" may not also involve what can be called a nonkerygmatic posture—that is, a stance on the part of the Christian which deliberately and meticulously *surrenders any claim to authority* [italics my own].
>
> It would seem that only in such a posture is genuine dialogue possible. . . . A claim to religious authority, carried into a dialogue however polite, is a club held under the table. A claim to authority always projects the point at which coercion will replace communication.[54]

It would be extremely unfair to imply that this earlier statement is at absolute variance with the opinions expressed in 1971, or to fail to note that an emphasis needed by the church at one time might not have changed in ten years. But the direction of the change is significant. Likewise, it illustrates the cycles of opinion to which proclamation is subjected, largely due to its own cycling between "authoritarianism" and "loss of nerve."

Anyone, with a little effort, can discover many other extensive references similar to these. What conclusion can we draw from this impressive testimony? What is it about preaching that causes it to be regarded with such seriousness?

Obviously each of these theologians would want to answer that question for himself. And their answers would be radically different, poles apart. But however the replies might be worded, two elements would appear to me to be indispensable to the answer: *preaching bears the eternal Word*, and *preaching touches the living situation*. That is, the historic given of the Christian faith encounters the experiential given of the contemporary situation through preaching. "Faith cometh by hearing" (Rom. 10:17), and "He that heareth you heareth me" (Luke 10:16).

Preaching is not essential to the church or to theology because the church has always done it, or because the early apostles did it, or even because Jesus did it. Preaching continues to have an irreplaceable position in Christian theology and Christian worship because it does what God did in his self-disclosure to Israel, in his revelation to prophets and apostles, in the fullness of his revelation in Jesus. It provides a medium for revelation which enables the eternal Word to maintain its living, dynamic character and encounter our concrete situation.

When the Word would make its fullness known, it took on flesh and dwelt among us; and in order to make itself known *now*, the Word must *keep on* becoming flesh among us. As we shall see, only when preaching is incarnational is it truly preaching.

It is not merely a parable to say that preaching "becomes flesh and dwells among us." The two determinative elements of revelation are present in that statement: the Word and the human situation. "The Word" speaks of God's gracious self-disclosure; "dwells among us" is the human dimension essential to our understanding. True preaching participates in both.

Preaching is often criticized for its inability to get people to *do* something—"people do not do something just because they are told." But this critique betrays a shallow concept of preaching and ultimately turns back on itself. That is, preaching is *not* "telling people what to do"[55]—although at its worst it degenerates into that. In preaching, Person comes to persons through person. Preaching is personal encounter, word-event, ongoing revelation.

The ultimate promise of language is not that it conveys *something* to us, but *someone*: "The Word as an event is always something said from one to another. . . . The Word which is concerned with God would then in this sense *say God to us*, so that *God comes to the one addressed and is with him*, and the one addressed is with God."[56] But if we promise ourselves to another, we lie. Even at our best we cannot fulfill that promise: "Only the Word by which God comes to man, and promises himself, is able to do this. That this Word has happened, and can therefore be spoken again and again, that a man can therefore promise God to another as the One who promises himself—this is the certainty of the Christian faith."[57]

God's Good News is no less that the promise of the Person who can, and will, come to the people. No one can do more for another than that.

Theology, then, takes preaching seriously because through it Christ comes to his people. The preacher who has the faith to believe that this is so can share the theologian's enthusiasm for preaching.

But hope is difficult to maintain in the face of frustrated experience, and the preacher may be forgiven if sometimes his own experience of preaching causes his faith to shrink smaller than the proverbial mustard seed. What is harder to believe than that my words can bear the divine Word? Little wonder that we stumble: "Lord, I believe; help thou mine unbelief!" Preaching is the ultimate act of faith.

The past two chapters have revealed at least two of the primary reasons for the double stubbornness of the pulpit. Its authentic Christian nature and the lofty promise accorded it by theology have kept it stubbornly there, but its stubborn unwillingness or inability to fulfill the promise of its heritage has subjected it to an increasing barrage of criticism. At its best, the stubbornness of the pulpit is the result of its hope. At its worst, the stubbornness of the pulpit is the result of its pride. Its pride, unless overcome, will kill it; its hope, unless misplaced, will save it. It is apparent that the recovery of its true voice is mandatory for the survival of the contemporary pulpit. But how?

3

TOWARD INCARNATIONAL PREACHING

The struggles of the early church against heresy principally involved the question of the nature of Christ. For centuries the ancient theological councils wrestled with the dialectic in the name *Jesus Christ: Jesus*—is he not the carpenter's son? And *Christ*—is he not the Promised One? Was he God, man, or Godman? How could the divine Word take on human flesh?

The early heresies made short work of that paradox. For some, like the Ebionites, he was a man, nothing more. He may have appeared to be divine, but he was not; his divinity was only imagined from his impressive humanity. For others, like the Docetics, he was divine, nothing less. He might have appeared to be human, but he was not; his humanity was only an accommodating illusion. In both heresies, the reality of the incarnation was denied.

These same dangers threaten proclamation. Preaching must recognize that it stands between the attraction of two powerful poles: to its right, "the faith once delivered," the historical given of the eternal Word; to its left, the present situation, the existential given of our own contemporary culture. Christian proclamation is intimately connected with both.

But preaching fails the dual promise accorded it by theology—that it bears the eternal Word, and that it touches the contemporary situation—when it betrays the wholeness of its calling by affirming part of its nature and denying the other. To the left, preaching becomes all human; to the right, all divine. To the left, there is nothing of God; to the right, there is nothing for man.

Even God himself had to become incarnate to communicate with man at the most profound level. The incarnation was the supreme revelation of God because it was God's ultimate means of communication. Nothing else could rival this ultimate revelation, that "God was in Christ," that "the Word was made flesh, and dwelt among us" (John 1:14), not even the history of his self-disclosure to Israel. Neither the historic pronouncements of the lawgivers nor the contemporary utterances of inspired prophets could approach the fullness of revelation of the incarnate Christ: "He that hath seen me hath seen the Father" (John 14:9).

The incarnation, therefore, is the truest theological model for preaching because it was God's ultimate act of communication. Jesus, who was the Christ, most perfectly said God to us because the eternal Word took on human flesh in a contemporary situation. Preaching cannot do otherwise.

But each of us as proclaimers is pulled between the poles, tempted to one heresy or the other due to personality, temperament, or confessional tradition. We are torn between the historical and the contemporary, the Word and culture, the human and the divine, objectivity and subjectivity, authoritarianism and autonomy. Every preacher should understand himself well enough to recognize the particular direction of this fierce pull upon his own preaching.

Is he fascinated with the smallest historic details in the Bible but uninterested in the largest current issues of his own time? Is Jerusalem more familiar territory to him than the avenues of his own hometown? Is he able to shed honest tears of compassionate understanding over the prodigals of the New Testament at the same time he is unable to do more than shake his fist at the prodigals on the highways of his own world?

Or on the other hand, is he intrigued by the contemporary scene but impatient with the ancient Word? Is he eager to find God in every contemporary movement but reluctant to identify

him in the historic revelation? Has the Bible become a virtual
embarrassment to his preaching while every contemporary
source is regarded as authoritative for it?

Like the early church, preaching is constantly tempted
toward incarnational heresy. But the Word must go on becoming flesh, and the preacher who succumbs to homiletical heresy
destroys any possibility of that happening.

Homiletical Heresy

On either side of the pulpit we are threatened by homiletical
heresies that stand left and right of incarnational preaching: to
the right, the preoccupation with the historic and the divine; to
the left, the preoccupation with the contemporary and the
human. This is the true split chancel of the church. To the
right, "Beware of the leaven of the Pharisees"; but likewise to
the left, "Beware of the leaven of the Sadducees" (Matt. 16:6).
Let us examine the dangers which each of these tendencies
poses for preaching.

The Leaven of the Pharisees

Jesus warned his disciples to "Beware of the leaven of the
Pharisees." That is, they were warned against losing themselves in legalistic preoccupation with the letter of the law. For
the Pharisees, nothing could rival the ancient law in importance. The books of the prophets were rarely used in the syn-
agogues; the writings, virtually never. Even the Messiah, when
he came, would do nothing more than interpret the law of
Moses. He could add nothing new; he could only interpret that
which was already written. It is little wonder that the freshness
of revelation which Jesus brought to the contemporary scene
met with fierce opposition from the Pharisees. The contemporary meant nothing; the historical meant everything.

This slavish devotion to the historical letter of the law
actually resulted from the Pharisee's fear of human fallibility.

Their memories of the Babylonian captivity were so bitter that they were fanatically determined to build a hedge about the Law to prevent the possibility of any future human intrusion. This same fear of the human factor soon manifested itself in Christian circles in the Docetism of the second century, which was another attempt to preserve the divine by eliminating the human.

The perpetuation of this error is a major source of the problems of preaching. Whenever the pulpit is not aware of the leaven of the Pharisees, it falls victim to a deadening legalism, homiletical Docetism, and cultural ghettoism. When preaching turns its back on the contemporary given, its own human involvement with the living situation, and exclusively embraces the pole of its historical given, then proclamation becomes partial, inadequate, and distorted.

Both the theological right and the theological left can be guilty of this error. It is not the exclusive property of any one theological position although this misunderstanding may manifest itself in different ways. But the basic problem is the same, and it exhibits two common traits.

First, *it fears the human factor.* This homiletical Docetism is afraid that the power of preaching will be lost or its message corrupted if it admits its humanity. Such fear results in a cult of objectivity. For the theological right, this fear usually manifests itself in a literalistic fundamentalism. The Bible "says what it means and means what it says." The necessity for interpretation may be denied altogether; all that is necessary is to "say what the Bible says." After all, if the preacher himself got involved in the process, how could he be certain that he was preaching God's absolute, objective truth?

But this same fault is exhibited in the preaching of men who are by no means fundamentalists. Neoorthodoxy has a particular problem at this point. About the only thing that can be said about the preacher's role in proclamation is that he needs to get out of the way. The writings of many theologians of this school, Barth's in particular, are filled with such expressions as "the Word arises out of the Bible," and "the preacher simply must not hinder its way into the congregation." These expressions reveal a false objectivity with reference to the preaching of the word. (Strictly speaking, Barth is a homiletical fundamentalist, as strange as that may seem. There is no position farther to the homiletical right than his. In fact, if the preacher were any less involved, he would simply have to stand mute at the pulpit while the Bible spoke for itself.)

Bonhoeffer also shows these tendencies. He speaks of the relief that comes to the preacher following the sermon when he is able to serve the Lord's Supper and know that something is occurring which does not depend upon his subjective involvement. It is apparent that the human factor is regarded as a minus in the preaching equation, a necessary evil at best.

It is extremely curious that men who would be the first to insist upon the reality of the humanity of Jesus should have such evident difficulty with the human element in the contemporary revelation of the Word. And theologians who would be the last to deny the human instrumentality of the writers of the biblical revelation should not be the first to fear the human instrumentality of the preacher of that revelation.

Second, *this homiletical heresy ignores its own cultural emphasis.* When Jesus preached, it was said that he "taught them as one having authority, and not as the scribes" (Matt. 7:29). What does that mean? Principally it implies that he did not speak in footnotes as the scribes did, endlessly drawing authority from previously recognized rabbis and thereby building his message from culturally accepted truisms. But this Scripture also reveals that the Pharisees, who purportedly scorned cultural influences and dealt only with the pure Law, were actually enslaved to their own cultural, inherited tradition. They overlooked their oral law which had become more important than the word of God itself.

The same was true of the Puritans. They purported to say nothing that the Bible did not say, but they actually created a body of human tradition that ranged far afield of the Bible. Likewise, the fundamentalist who "only says what the Bible says" obviously does not merely stand in the pulpit reading the

Bible aloud. He is actually transmitting a body of culturally inherited dogma—usually from oral tradition—without realizing it, and all of his statements from the pulpit which are not direct quotations of Scripture are human interpretations, theological statements from his own tradition. Not only do most of these statements have difficulty finding their way back to biblical origins, many of them actually do not date beyond the preacher's own grandfather.

The more critically enlightened positions on the homiletical right, such as neoorthodoxy, also cannot escape their cultural environment. Every act of interpretation carries with it an entire body of inherited presuppositions and subjective statements. No informed theology would deny that, but it is inconsistent to admit it readily with reference to theological affirmations made in the study and attempt to minimize it when those same affirmations are made from the pulpit.

Let us be quite honest about this. There is a touch of magic here, as if God mysteriously grants a man the ability to be less subjective in his preaching than he is in his writing. The passionate desire to insure that the pure word of God is proclaimed to the congregation has resulted in an almost superstitious depersonalization of the act of preaching. As a matter of practical fact, the Word does not "arise out of the Bible and proceed into the congregation." It proceeds into the congregation on the words of a very subjective human being who has struggled to interpret those words which he has found in the Bible and which God graces with his presence as the Word.

This one-sided emphasis on the historical given of Christian proclamation, particularly in its less-informed expressions, has produced several interesting and quite specific results:

(1) *Extreme emphasis on the original language of the text.* For some preachers this has meant nothing more than a careful attention to exegesis, with perhaps some overemphasis on historical footnoting in the sermon, but in other cases it has resulted in the various dictation theories of inspiration. Because the human element is so feared, these mechanical theories had to be concocted in order to protect the transmis-

sion of the word from human instrumentality. This is the reason that the expression, "inspired in the autographs" is so popular among some groups, and also why the most extremely conservative theological seminaries devote such a preponderance of the curriculum to original language studies. There is safety in the original, literal words; there is danger in the interpretation of them. In this case, "the spirit killeth, but the letter bringeth life."

Elaborate, rigid grammatical systems also have been devised as a mechanical means for arriving at correct interpretation. This slide-rule method of solving all questions of interpretation attempts to achieve an impersonal, objective—and therefore infallible—statement of the meaning of the Bible.

(2) *A reliance upon cultic language.* Since the preacher who is involved in this heresy eventually realizes that he cannot simply "preach the Bible" (unless he does nothing more than read the Bible aloud from the pulpit), but that he must use his own fallible human words, he takes another step to remove the human element from his preaching. He employs cultic language, language formulas handed down by his tradition. Then he cannot be held accountable for his words since even when he is not quoting Scripture he is also not using his own words but the words given to him by his tradition.

This cultic language may express itself in the conventional clichés of a language of Zion, or the more sophisticated formulations of a neolanguage of Zion, the most updated terminology for expressing one's faith "with integrity." But in both cases an oral tradition is being followed. And some groups who pride themselves upon having "no creeds from men" which influence their preaching have instead an oral tradition of dogma and language far more rigid and intimidating than any written creed.

(3) *The use of a "holy tone" in delivery.* In addition to trying to excuse himself from the preaching formula through a reliance upon mechanical inspiration and cultic language, the preacher makes one final attempt to completely objectify the preaching experience. He relies upon a voice whose tone and cadence mark it as something definitely more than human.

The famous "ministerial tune" is another attempt at false objectification, the last weapon in the minister's arsenal of defenses against human involvement in preaching. The sing-song cadence of the ministerial tune and the orotund tone of the ministerial voice betray the insecurity of the preacher who wants to hide from his personal responsibility in proclaiming the word.

As Bonhoeffer has pointed out, this false objectivity in preaching may even yearn for its liturgical ancestor, the Latin language of the Catholic Mass (which *really* obscured the human component); or it may move steadily toward music as a more objective and therefore less vulnerable medium for the word. The contemporary spoken word is not good enough for the holy act of worship; a chanted tone must be employed. Bonhoeffer cites the liturgical chants of the Middle Ages as an example. *The ministerial tune is the medieval chant of Protestant worship.* By falling into the singing cadence, the preacher subconsciously is striving to further objectify his words so that they will not seem so subjective.

The errors of this extreme objectivism are pathetic efforts to insure that nothing but the divine occurs in preaching, no matter how human the body of proclamation might appear to be. But at the opposite pole, the contemporary or existential given of the preaching task, a second homiletical heresy tempts the preacher: an emphasis upon the contemporary and the human to the exclusion of the historical and the divine.

The Leaven of the Sadducees

The Pharisees were ill at ease with their contemporary, pluralistic culture, but the Sadducees certainly were not. They were eager to embrace the Hellenistic culture of their modern era, to wear the Greek hat and hurl the javelin. The Sadducees were as willing to conform to culture as the Pharisees were determined to ignore it.

Likewise, in Christian circles the desire to relate to the contemporary, no matter what the cost, was not long in surfacing. This tendency found its most extreme expression in the Montanism of the second century. Montanus and his followers believed that they had received direct revelation from God apart from any historical connection whatsoever. Their delusion became so extreme, in fact, that Montanus finally believed himself to be none other than the Holy Spirit.

These tendencies are very much a part of the contemporary scene for preaching. Because of our "recent bad history" of authoritarianism and absolutism in the pulpit, we fear the leaven of the Pharisees extraordinarily. The past few decades have witnessed an era of overreaction to literalism, legalism, and extreme Puritanism. As a result, preaching has been lured into cultural accommodation and a "too-easy peace with culture," to use Niebuhr's term; or what Peter Berger has referred to as "culture Protestantism." Berger has been sharply critical of the tendency to make "modern man" and "modern consciousness" into "golden calves around which a depressing number of Christian thinkers have staged an ongoing dance celebration"; and he has described "the more bizarre exaggerations of religious accommodation to the modern spirit" as having reached the point of absurdity.[1]

The influence of contemporary culture is an inescapable reality for the preacher. He cannot deny the human factor in his preaching. His ministry has a specific cultural setting; he himself is very much the product of it and so is the congregation to whom he speaks. But if he becomes preoccupied with an immediate revelation, with contemporary visions which divorce his bit of history from the historic revelation of God, then his preaching falls prey to homiletical Montanism.

What are the characteristics of this error? Precisely the opposite of the one-sided emphasis on the historical dimension of preaching.

(1) *It emphasizes immediacy of revelation.* The biblical revelation is virtually ignored in homiletical Montanism; the key question becomes, "How do *I* understand God?" The self-appointed, popular prophetic figure is just as dangerous to the church regardless of which side of the theological stage he stands upon. This is true of the wildly apocalyptic preacher

who ignores the historic meanings of the biblical images he tortures into contorted shapes; but it is equally true of the sophisticated preacher who believes that the Bible is hopelessly irrelevant and that revelation is the product of his own enlightened self-understanding.

We must test the spirits; and if they do not speak of Jesus Christ, they are not of the Spirit of God. *Without the humility which places it beneath the Word, only the demonic can and will occur in preaching.*

(2) *It exaggerates the human factor.* If homiletical Docetism fears the human factor, homiletical Montanism is intoxicated with it. It believes that if anything is going to happen in preaching, the preacher must *make* it happen. Therefore this preaching is success-oriented. It strives for effect. It constantly holds a mirror before its face to see how attractive it is.

In its cruder forms, this preaching is deliberately and consciously manipulative; in its more sophisticated forms, it is subtly intimidating in its cultural correctness. Its insecurity may drive it into a restless search for innovative forms—not to better communicate the gospel, but to please its crowd—just as the rhyming sermons of Wycliff's day were intended to entertain and gain popular approval.

(3) *It ignores its own dependence on authority.* Because this preaching is so humanistic, it prefers to believe that it is not authoritarian. In an age of rapid change, certainty is an embarrassment and ambiguity a pride. Sophistication and ambiguity are twins. But sophistication is knowing, and so is ambiguity. Ambiguity is knowing what not to know. This is merely another subtle and powerful kind of authoritarianism.

It is amazing how oblivious this preaching is to its own desperate search for authority. For the sophisticated, "progressive" preacher, this need is usually satisfied by fact-stacking and contemporary authority-citing. On the other hand, the "conservative" preacher who has in fact actually abandoned the authority of the Word attempts to fill this void by endlessly citing personal experiences, either his own or those of others. The word of God is largely ignored in this kind of preaching;

our experiences become the authority for the sermon. It is
fearful preaching, too; fearful that without this constant experi-
ence-mongering, God disappears. Primitive religion always
lacks faith and therefore demands miraculous experiences.
Miracle-mongering, likewise, whether of the Shantung revival
or of medieval Catholicism, reveals the same anxiety—that
without such human proofs, the Word is impotent.

Even the noble insistence upon the "priesthood of the
believer," the belief in the competency of the individual to
interpret the Bible for himself, can lead to self-pride and a
distorted sense of authority. This invariably occurs when anyone arrogantly insists on his subjective rights and refuses to
listen to the testimony of the historic word but instead brings
his previously held notions to it, and then comes forth proclaiming the accuracy of his cultural totems. In this case, the
"priest" ceases to be priest and becomes God.

More could be said about each of these extremes, but perhaps
this description will help us to identify the dangers of homiletical extremism.

I would hope that one thing is now clear. Neither the historical nor the contemporary, the Bible or man, is served by these
distortions. The Pharisee believed himself to be faithful to the
law and above the dangers of cultural corruption, but in fact he
made both himself and the law captive to the oral traditions of
his own culture. And the Sadducee merely added a thin cultural veneer over his own rigidly legalistic interpretation of
life.

The same is true today. Those preachers who seek to save the
word of God from the human and the contemporary merely
lock it up in some human tradition from the past, which is no
more sacred or less human because it is hallowed by time. But
likewise some preachers who wish to escape the archaic stance
of biblical authoritarianism really betray the contemporary by
their legalistic insistence upon the new "right" way of saying
things. The tragedy of these one-sided efforts is that in both
cases the communication of the living Word to the living
situation never happens.

To be sure, neither of these, the Pharisee or the Sadducee, actually exists in such broad portraits. But each of us participates enough in one or the other of them—or both—to know that these figures are real, and let the one who thinks that he stands at balanced midpoint take heed lest he fall.

The Two Poles

I have tried to demonstrate that preaching, like all of theology, is pulled between two powerful poles of attraction: God and man, the human and the divine, the Creator and his creation. All of our other terms of classification—liberal and conservative, left and right, the historical and the contemporary— are usually only means of describing a dominant emphasis on one or the other of these poles.

So whether we refer to the homiletical right, or the historical pole for preaching, we are referring to the attempt of proclamation to be faithful to the divine dimension of its character. Conversely, to speak of the homiletical left, or the contemporary pole of preaching, is to refer to·proclamation's efforts to be faithful to its humanity.

There is a positive value for us in the negative study of the heresies which result when preaching becomes a divided self. We realize that both of these extremes have seized upon something essential to the nature of proclamation.

The homiletical right has grasped the importance of the historic revelation, of the priority of the actions of God, and of the confrontation of contemporary culture with the word of God. The homiletical left has realized that preaching is a ministry which God has graciously given to his human servants, that it must speak to the actual needs of the real people of its own time, and therefore that it must have a sensitivity to people and a willingness to experiment with contemporary means of communicating with them. The right sees the importance of the historical and the divine; the left sees the value of the contemporary and the human.

But no preaching can be truly whole, and therefore truly itself, until it has thoroughly committed itself to *both* of these realities. This means that an incarnational approach to preaching must be based upon two primary affirmations: *first, that Christian proclamation recognizes the priority of the actions of God;* and *second, that Christian proclamation recognizes the possibility of the irrelevance of the preaching of men.* Let us examine each of these affirmations.

(1) *Christian proclamation recognizes the priority of the actions of God.* God has acted. He has acted in Israel; he has acted in Christ. Christian speaking begins with the speaking of God; we speak because we have been addressed. Our preaching does not merely speak of our own subjective inquiry, *but it is based upon the reality which was brought to light in the actions of God.*

In referring to the preaching of the apostles concerning the resurrection, Jürgen Moltmann writes: "They did not merely wish to tell of their own new self-understanding in the Easter faith, but in that faith and as a result of it they reported something also about the way of Jesus and about the event of the raising of Jesus. Their statements contain not only existential certainty in the sense of saying, 'I am certain,' but also and together with this objective certainty in the sense of saying, 'It is certain.'"[2]

This does not mean that we are committed to a mere historical recital in preaching (nor that historical "proof" is either possible or essential), but that preaching will seek to express that reality which was brought to light in the prior revealing actions of God.

(2) *Christian proclamation recognizes the possibility of the irrelevance of the preaching of men.* Contemporary preaching has already wasted far too much time in the pointless debate on whether or not the word of God "has to be made relevant." How could a word from God be irrelevant?

But we will avoid a great deal of lost motion if we direct ourselves to another question. Is all preaching invariably the word of God? And therefore, is all preaching invariably rele-

vant? Does the word of God invariably encounter me every time
the preacher mounts the pulpit steps and opens his mouth, no
matter what he says to me or how I am addressed?

Obviously not. This means that there is a real human dimension to proclamation and that the question of relevance is
inescapably bound up with it. *The preaching of the word of
God is the interpretation of a historical event to a contemporary situation by a man who must be intimately familiar with
both.* Any separation on the part of the preacher from either of
these situations results in irrelevant preaching.

If my preaching does not understand the reality revealed in
the historic word of God, it cannot speak to the ultimate needs
of my contemporary congregation. But if I am alienated from
my own times so that I cannot understand the unique language
with which the contemporary expresses its alienation from
God, then I cannot find understandable words to speak the
historic revelation: "As God in Christ entered into a specific
culture at a given time and place, so the message of the revela-
tory-redemptive act must become incarnate in and for each
generation by entering the culture of that generation and
redeeming it."[3]

The word of God is never irrelevant, but my preaching may
well be. And it will be, if it does not bear the eternal Word, and
if it does not touch the living situation. Only the word which
dwells among us is the word of Christian preaching.

Midpoint: Communication

But it is not enough simply to set the two poles of the
historical given and the contemporary given of Christian proclamation and to assert that they are both important. We must
also ask how they are related. This is the essential problem for
Christian preaching: "Christianity, whether defined as church,
creed, ethics or movement of thought, itself moves between the
poles of Christ and culture. The *relation* of these two consti-
tutes the problem."[4]

What is the relationship between these two poles? In other words, what assurance can the preacher have that the "square peg" of the ancient word will fit the round hole of contemporary needs?

The preacher must understand that the historic word and the contemporary situation are not mutually exclusive and that preaching unites the two in the act of communication. These are the two primary guideposts toward incarnational preaching: the first points to *what* is preached, to the message itself; the second, to the *act* of preaching. Each requires some attention.

1. *The historic word and the contemporary situation are not mutually exclusive.* Preaching must not allow itself to be forced into a false antithesis between the objective and the subjective, between the word and men.[5] Subjective preaching invariably results in the cultivation of men; objective preaching invariably results in the coercion of men. But *subjective* and *objective* are really useless terms for the preacher because of the unity between the "objective" word and the "subjective" congregation.

The contemporary preacher must realize that the congregation he addresses is already present in the word of God in the Bible: "When the Bible lies open on the preacher's desk and the preparation of the sermon is about to begin, the worshipers have already come in; the passage contains these people since it is God's word to his people."[6] The subjective congregation is already present in the objective word because it is the word of God to men.

Not only is the congregation present in the word, however, but what the word offers is precisely what the congregation needs. Man was created in the image of God. His emptiness is his alienation from God, and all of his incompleteness, whether he realizes it or not, is the result of the absence of the word.

If the word and men were related as objective and subjective, as philosophical absolutes, then there would be no hope for preaching at all. After all, why should the contemporary preacher go to the Bible in the first place? What hope does he have that the ancient record contains a message for his contemporary congregation? And what hope does he have that the message preached is the message needed? But he is able to believe that the word addresses all men in all cultural situations and at all times—even his own contemporary congregation—when he understands the essential human dimensions in the provision of the word, and the essential eternal dimension in the needs of men.

There are *three implications* from this understanding of the essential unity of the word and men for the Christian message:

(a) *The preacher must correctly positionize himself relative to the word.* We have already affirmed the priority of the actions of God. "It is he that hath made us, and not we ourselves" (Ps. 100:3). The same must be true of the Christian message.

The preacher himself must stand beneath the word he preaches, not above it. To stand above the word means to reject it, to ignore its message for ourselves, or to use it to manipulate men for our own ends. Then the essential order in proclamation is reversed, and we become the lord rather than the servant of the word. We violate both the essential nature of our humanity and God's sovereignty when we do not stand beneath the word.

To stand beneath the word means that we must acknowledge our own humanity. To acknowledge our humanity is to confess our sinfulness. To confess our sinfulness is to make plain to the congregation that we stand beneath the very judgment of the word we proclaim.

(b) *The preaching of the word demands a partial participation in culture.* Just as the preacher may take a false stance relative to the word, so he may also positionize himself incorrectly in relation to culture.

It is possible to be both overimpressed and underimpressed with culture. Being overimpressed with culture causes the preacher and his message to be dominated by it; being underimpressed with culture causes the preacher and his message to ignore it. Where culture has dominated, the ultimate significance of proclamation has been lost; where culture has been ignored, true communication of the message has been lost.

Preaching that is overly impressed with culture becomes weak and despairing and therefore incurs the scorn of the world. Preaching that is underimpressed with culture becomes arrogant and pharisaical, remote and cultic, and therefore incurs the hatred of the world.

The sermon is to have a note of certainty and joy. It is also to be prophetic. Neither of these notes can be sounded when preaching is overimpressed with culture. That is the reason for the failure of the world-weary and uncertain preacher. And conversely, it is the reason for the success of some fraudulent and simplistic preachers. Their prophetic certainty and joy may be feigned, but they are perceived as men who will confront the world with the declaration of the gospel.

Nevertheless, no truly prophetic preaching can ever occur, or has ever occurred, unless the preacher sufficiently participates in his culture to understand its unique language and respond understandably.

The solution to this dilemma is a *partial participation* in culture on the part of the preacher. If we did not participate at all in our culture, it would be impossible to communicate with it: "Communication is a matter of participation. Where there is no participation there is no communication."[7] But if there is an absolute identification of the preacher and his message with his contemporary culture, then the Christian gospel is lost in a capitulation to culture: "We can speak to people only if we participate in their concern. . . . We can point to the Christian answer only if, on the other hand, we are not identical with them."[8]

This partial participation in culture on our part permits the communication of the Christian message and a confrontation of culture: "We must participate but we must not be identical, and we must use this double attitude to undercut the complacency of those who assume that they know all the answers and are not aware of their existential conflicts."[9] Or, as Wingren has put it, "The priest may venture to belong to his own age and mix in the ordinary life of society without thereby losing the divine life. . . . When preaching willingly concerns itself with the needs and problems of its time, there takes place once more what ought to take place: Christ sits at the table with publicans and sinners, that is, with us. In the human, the divine is present."[10]

(c) *The subjectivity of our existence is a blessing rather than a curse, and so is the objectivity of the word.* For some preachers, the subjectivity of their existence is viewed as a liability, a handicap in the task of preaching. For others, the objectivity of the historical revelation, the particularity of the Word becoming flesh in the history of Israel and in the person of Jesus, is regarded as an ongoing hindrance to contemporary communication. Both of these stances are false.

In the first place, without my personal, subjective involvement with my congregation, with my culture, with these people here and now, I could not communicate at all. Preaching would be more futile than a Bedouin trying to describe a camel to an Eskimo, or an Eskimo attempting to describe a walrus to a Bedouin, when neither spoke the language of the other.

I do not enjoy many advantages over the apostle Paul, but there is one unique advantage which is mine: I am here and now, and he is not. And if the reality which he expressed in his life and in his theology is to come forth for my congregation, it will only be because his language and symbols have been translated and interpreted meaningfully for our time.

Just as transliteration of language is not adequate translation of the Bible, mere historical recital is not adequate proclamation of the gospel. Of course my subjective participation in culture and my interpretation of the Bible presents risks and dangers; but nevertheless, the subjectivity of my contemporary existence is a permit for preaching, not a prohibition of it.

Likewise, the preacher who feels himself limited by the historical given of revelation does not understand the facts of the case. It is *because* God particularized himself in Israel and in Jesus of Nazareth that we may have confidence in addressing the particular situation of the here and now. The God we proclaim is not abstract; he is not embarrassed to be involved in history; he is not too impersonal to enter into the sufferings of every human life.

And if I did not know that God exists as his Word quite apart from my own human understanding and fallibilities, as a preacher I should be of all men most miserable. Then the communication of the gospel would be entirely a matter of my own persuasive abilities, of my own sweaty exertions in the pulpit. But when I know that the presence of the Word in my preaching is entirely a matter of the sovereign grace of God, then I may have a confidence that transcends self-confidence. Then I may commit my preaching to his promise and rest my trust in him.

2. *The historic word and the contemporary situation become united in the act of communication.* This is the second of our guideposts toward incarnational preaching. Again, the incarnational model demonstrates the truthfulness of this claim.

(a) *Speech was an essential part of the communication of the human and the divine in the incarnation of Jesus.* The words of Jesus apart from his life would have been empty; but the life of Jesus apart from his words would have been unintelligible. We cannot imagine a mute, silent Jesus. The Good News apart from words is inconceivable. Perpetual silence from Jesus could only have led to ambiguity; speech led to the cross. None of his deeds, neither the miraculous nor the compassionate, could have unmistakably said God to us apart from the interpretation which his words provide. "Never man spake like this man" (John 7:46); and with all of our difficulties in interpreting those words, imagine the confusion we would suffer apart from them.

Speech connected him to the inner being of men. Beyond everything men could observe in his actions, the words of Jesus identified with hurts in the human spirit and ministered to them at those subtle depths of the human predicament where hands can no longer reach. And at this depth, we find him most identified with our humanity; but paradoxically, it is also in this dimension that we realize most fully that he is God.

True, there were times when Jesus was silent—as before

Pilate, when every word might appear to be a plea for deliverance. Then he would not allow words to be misunderstood as a capitulation of the Word to culture; then he was silent. But silence was never normative for his ministry.

That is not surprising to us because silence is never normative for a human being. Nor is it for the church as the body of Christ. Speech is indeed the greatest danger of the church because it is the most human. "Language is the basic cultural creation" of man; and whether the symbols used are silent or spoken, "every act of man's spiritual life is carried by language."[11] Words are wily. Potential. But human. This leads us to a second implication:

(b) *Speech is an essential part of the communication of the Word by the church.* As the body of Christ, the human church has form, it acts and it speaks. Its form is uncomely because it is human—it is not God, nor angel, nor even intermediate being. It acts and fails because it is human. It confesses its sinfulness and acts again. So when it speaks and fails, it must also speak again. God does not refuse himself to his church even in its weakness and its humanity, and the Word does not deny itself to the fallibility of human speech. "A bruised reed shall he not break, and the smoking flax shall he not quench . . ." (Isa. 42:3; Matt. 12:20).

The nervousness of the church over its proclamation is partly proper and partly false: partly proper because it correctly recognizes its frequent failures and often abuse of the office of preaching; partly false because it realizes that the explicitness and concreteness of speech will make clear the distinctiveness of the gospel. It is good that the church fears its former exaggerations (it has said too much, and it has caused men to stumble over itself).

But the church cannot simply act and leave its actions in ambiguity. A speechless, formless, disembodied church is a heresy. True, it is not as risky—but it is also not as human. The risk of humanness was essential to the incarnation, and there is no true humanness without speech.

Furthermore, without speech the church cannot reveal the divine source of its life. Just because we are not God, none of us can perfectly incarnate the Word in our deeds. We must always point beyond ourselves with words to the fullness of the revelation of God. And with all of the serious difficulties the church faces in finding suitable language to speak of God, it really has no other choice: "The Biblical faith . . . must speak of God. . . . A God to whom human words cannot point is not the God of the Bible."[12]

Since the word of God is intended, in Brunner's words, to "make himself accessible to me," and "the sole analogy is the encounter between human beings, the meeting with person with persons," then the spoken word is especially suited for the communication of that word.[13] It is "right within the core of the I-thou relationship, and the written or printed word is always a poor substitute for it."[14] In fact, Kyle Haselden has made the bold assertion that in the presentation of the gospel, "the spoken word is the best weapon, the superlative tool; in this area it has superiority over all other forms of communication."[15]

This suggests our final conclusion concerning the speech of the church:

(c) *Proper speech is essential to overcome the wrong stumbling block to the gospel, our inability to communicate.* But it is at this point that theology begins to raise its red flags of warning. Eberhard Bethge says that Dietrich Bonhoeffer never asked, "How can we better communicate to modern man the message we possess? That question would turn the interpreter into a salesman to the have-nots."[16] This suspicion of any studied approach to the oral communication of the gospel is widespread in theology.

In an article entitled, "Theology vs. Communication Theories," Ronald E. Sleeth lists six current criticisms of theology at this point: (1) Theology has expressed its disapproval of the application of communication theories to preaching by ignoring them; (2) this indifference is actually based upon the fear that the study of oral communication elevates the human and minimizes the divine; (3) theology regards the task of communication as a theological one, and it sees communication theory as affirming that right techniques rightly learned are sufficient for communicating the message of the gospel; (4) theology is suspicious of communication because of its apparent instrumental or pragmatic use of the religious message; (5) theologians are afraid of the study of communication because of their fear of manipulation; (6) theology is concerned about the humanistic implications of some speech theories because of their preoccupation with the behavioral and social sciences.[17]

These are warnings not to be ignored. We can readily agree with Tillich when he says, "The question cannot be: How do we communicate the Gospel so that others will accept it? For this there is no method. To communicate the Gospel means putting it before the people so that they are able to decide for or against it. . . . All that we who communicate this Gospel can do is to make possible the genuine decision."[18]

But must we not also agree with Tillich when he says that there are two kinds of "stumbling blocks" in Christianity: "One is genuine. . . . There is always a genuine decision against the gospel for those for whom it is a stumbling block. But this decision should not be dependent upon the wrong stumbling block, namely, the wrong way of our communication of the gospel—our inability to communicate." He insists that this wrong stumbling block must be overcome in order to bring people face to face with the right stumbling block, the gospel itself, and he asks, "Will the Christian churches be able to remove the wrong stumbling blocks in their attempt to communicate the gospel?"[19]

In other words, Tillich is saying that communication does not mean persuasion; that is, even if a man says *no* to the gospel, it has still been communicated—*if* it is the gospel he is rejecting, and not merely our presentation of it. But it has not been communicated if he never gets to the gospel at all because he has stumbled over my presentation of it.

If Tillich is right at this point, and I believe that he is, then this has important implications for the responsible involvement of theology in the practical dimensions of preaching. If our methods of communicating the gospel can set a false stumbling block in the paths of men so that they are never able to hear the gospel at all, *then our presentation of the message is*

*an essential part of the contemporary hearing of the living
Word.*

No theologian would argue that an unstudied exposition of a
biblical text is superior to one which gives careful attention to
the text in light of the most recent contributions of critical
research and modern hermeneutical theories. But is it not
utterly contradictory of theology to insist that it is our right—
indeed, our absolute responsibility—to use the best of recent
research in arriving at the proper *interpretation* of the Christian message, and yet to object to the use of the best of recent
research in arriving at a proper *presentation* of the Christian
message?

Theology must realize that an understanding of communication is to the presentation of the sermon what critical research
is to the content of the sermon. And with the same attendant
benefits and dangers. Critical research helps the preacher in the
interpretation of the Christian message; communication theory
helps the preacher in the presentation of the Christian message.

Of course there are dangers in the use of communication
theory, just as in the use of critical research. But how are these
dangers to be avoided? Do we avoid false interpretation by
refusing to study the principles of interpretation? Is a spontaneous interpretation free of error? Likewise, can we prevent
manipulation in the act of preaching by an unstudied, spontaneous presentation? Or is my involvement simply not needed
in the pulpit? When I stand to speak, does the divine immediately take over?

If not, then theology must give more attention to the practical
act of preaching if Christian proclamation is to be made whole.

How then can theology inform practical homiletics? The
reality of the historic word and the contemporary situation
must become incarnate in the man who preaches, in the shape
of the sermon which he preaches, and in the language with
which he preaches.

But we must begin with the man. If these realities are not
incarnate in him, they can never become incarnated in his
preaching.

4

"WE ARE MEN LIKE YOURSELVES"

The greatest confession of the early church was the Caesarean confession of Simon, "Thou art the Christ, the Son of the living God" (Matt. 16:16). But if that is its greatest confession, the Lyconian confession of the Apostle Paul ranks second only to it: "We are men like yourselves . . ." (Acts 14:15). In fact, no man can make that exalted confession of Simon without first having made this contrite confession of Paul, "We are men . . ."

For the preacher, this Lyconian confession takes on added significance. Without it, he can never point beyond himself or escape the despair which playing God brings. Sooner or later in life, we will all make this confession. It may come as a shattering realization or as a buried neuroticism, but it will come. It may come early in life, with life's first frustrations and failures; or it may come with the assumption of family responsibilities, or the disappointments of ambition or career, or the crises of the thirties or the fears of the forties; or with gathering years and declining health—or with death—but it will come. Unfortunately most of life is spent either in the postponement of this confession or in the self-deception that it is not true. Nothing could be more destructive to Christian ministry.

To understand how this is so, look at the experiences of Paul and Barnabas in Lyconia which produced this confession. They had healed a crippled man by the gate. The priests of Jupiter had tried to crown them with garlands, thinking that the gods had finally fulfilled all the old legends and come down to earth in the form of men. Then Paul rent his clothes and ran into the midst of the excited crowd, shouting, "Stop! Why are you doing these things? We are men like yourselves, and we are here to tell you of the true and living God whom we serve." But the Scripture says, "Even with these words they scarcely restrained the crowd from worshiping them" (Acts 14:8–22).

Imagine, however, what would have happened if Paul and Barnabas had not confessed their humanity. At first their authority would have been infinitely greater. Huge crowds would have gathered to see them. Of course there would have been demands—healing, miraculous displays, prophetic visions. They could have concealed their humanity and stalled, reminding the throngs of the last wonder and promising more. And that would have satisfied the mob—for awhile. But sooner or later there would have come that knock on the door which said, "Produce—or else."

Then what? Theudas, who disappointed his hoard of avid followers by failing to collapse the walls of Jerusalem as promised and was stoned to death for his failure, was not the last religious figure to learn the penalty for playing god.

Humanity: Preventing Despair

Confessing his humanity is the only way the preacher can prevent complete despair in his ministry. Only when he can say, "I am a man; I am human. I can make mistakes; I can fail," is he able to eliminate the burden of divinity. That burden is simply to heavy to bear. No minister really thinks of himself as God. A few, perhaps, may regard themselves as a little more than human. According to reliable reports, at least one or two have been seen traveling with their feet a few inches above the ground.

A particularly adroit preacher may get away with this masquerade for a brief time—particularly if he moves frequently— but eventually his clay toes will peep out from his dusty sandals. Then his authority disappears along with his divinity, and both he and his followers are destroyed by the unmasking.

This error is particularly pernicious in the immature younger godling with a gigantic ego who has been bragged on too much because he is a ninety-day statistical wonder, or because he is a wizard at lay manipulation through psychological tricks. But "maturity" also tends to promote pride. The longer a preacher lives and works in churches, the more decisions he must make. So he makes them, and some of them even turn out right. He gains the approval of his religious culture; he is "successful." And after awhile, unless he is careful, he makes a very slight error: He confuses his words with the divine word, his will with God's will.

When the prophetic mantle falls on some men, it drops right over their heads. They can see neither the people nor the word of God.

I will not debate whether pride (hubris) or sloth (acedia) is the chief sin of the ministry. (As a matter of fact where there is one there is frequently the other.) But in its extreme forms, there is nothing worse than pride. It often shows itself in the arrogance of the word manipulator whose speech and dress exploit the insecurities of his middle-class or working congre- gation until he becomes a demigodling whose piousness and pompousness God himself would not use (and did not, in Christ). Or it may show itself in the arrogance of the subtle cynic whose speech and dress exploit the insecurities of his upper-class or intellectual congregation until he is the ultimate Man whose hypersophistication and blasé ways are the envy of his self-established in-cult with its obscure symbolism and new holy-language, which God himself would not use ("and the common people heard him gladly" [Mark 12:37]).

But in spite of their apparent differences both are brothers, sick brothers, sick unto death, leaving sickness in the wake and making their converts (not God's) tenfold more children of hell than before. If the light that shines from these windows, either stained-glass traditional or contemporary abstract, be darkness, how great is that darkness!

Both god-players find immense personal gratification in their cults; both scorn the opposite social pole; both attract fanatical personal allegiance from their followers whose insecurities are at last gratified by a superego which interprets all of life for them. And hell hath no fury like the cult-follower whose living space is intruded upon.

Needless to say, both would-be deities also build "great" churches or audiences, at least for a time. But people's taste in gods—when there is more than one—is notoriously fickle, and at the first sign of failure or fatigue on his part they are off, racing after the latest phenomenon to alleviate their lifeless boredom and give them the "spiritual" thrill they once felt. Meanwhile the dropped divinity may struggle all the more frantically to regain his niche by using ever cheaper and shabbier tricks. At this point, despair knows no lower depths, not even in Dante's lowest levels of hell.

The mob that worships most often stones when its gods fail them. That crowd which shouted "Hosanna!" to Jesus was yelling "Crucify him, crucify him!" next. He had frustrated their misguided expectations. Or the prodigal son with his carousing friends—where were they when he wandered about begging and finally crawled into a pigsty? Let the godlings who play roles and who pretend to be God fail and see what will happen.

Many Christian workers are obsessed with the terror of inconsistency: "What if I can't produce?" "What if giving or attendance fall below last year's?" "What if the next church goes *down* instead of *up*?" Such is the fear of the man who wears the mask of God, and behind it is a very human, frightened, insecure man. It will destroy him if he has the least shred of integrity, and it will destroy any church or denomination that becomes deluded by this pretension.

But when the minister confesses his humanity, he alleviates the fear of inconsistency. No matter how alluring the role of local divinity, deep inside every minister knows himself to be both human and fallible, empowered only by the Spirit of God. When he is able to confess that to himself and others, he can end the anxiety of the divine masquerade.

But confessing his humanity is not only essential to prevent the despair of the minister, it is also crucial for another reason. It is the only stance which permits our complete testimony to God.

Humanity: Permitting Testimony

Paul and Barnabas never could have witnessed to the true and living God if they had masqueraded as gods. But when they admitted their humanity, they were simultaneously set free to point beyond themselves to God. Paul said, "We are not here to be worshiped, but that you should turn from these meaningless things to serve the true and living God" (Acts 14:15). Curiously enough, when we most accept our humanity, we are most enabled to participate in the divine task.

This issue is so profound for the ministry that we must not be the least uncertain about it. As preachers of the incarnate Word, we must involve ourselves in incarnational preaching. We must be committed to the historical word and the contemporary world. Without the word, we have no message. Without the world, we have no ministry.

The insecurity of some preachers will not allow them to confess their humanity. The insecurity of other preachers will not allow them to admit their involvement with the divine. Both are afraid of their ministry groups, and both fall into a heresy of ministry.

That is, without a recognition of his humanity the preacher is condemned to deception, frustration, and depression. Feelings of guilt always result in depression. When a preacher tries to carry the burden of divinity and inevitably fails, he feels guilty and is dropped into depression, sometimes minor and transitory but sometimes extremely serious and disabling.

On the other hand, without a recognition that he is a child of God, a disciple, a joint heir with Christ and a part of his body, a preacher is likewise frustrated and depressed. He may be human enough—but what is the basis for his ministry? Without a steady confidence in his calling of God, in the guidance of

God's hand in his life, and the assurance of a strength beyond his own, his sense of purpose gradually erodes until he is baffled, depressed, and bored.

The boredom of the ministry—and it is at epidemic proportions—can be traced directly to spiritual sickness. No one who has a sense of vital, useful purpose can be bored except for normal periods of mental or physical fatigue. Any preacher who says he has never experienced such periods of boredom or depression is either manic or dishonest, or both. Even the most purposive routine is still routine, and eventually it gets repetitious and tedious.

But this occasional boredom is different from the settled, aching misery that some ministers struggle to live with. This emptiness of life, however, is precisely that which the coming of Christ was intended to fill: "I am come that they may have life, and that more abundantly" (John 10:10). Does not this promise apply also to Christ's ministers? Accepting one's humanity does not mean accepting a life of boredom in ministry. On the contrary, true humanity, humanity as it ought to be, is always in Christ, and the life in Christ is not one of boredom.

Nor, it should be added, is it one of perpetual excitement. The highly artificial happiness-cult in the church is spurious Christianity, and the preacher who perpetually tries to see how many upper teeth he can show in one smooth movement of the mouth does neither himself nor his congregation a favor. The kingdom does not come with much grinning. Rather than conquering depression and boredom, this pose only deepens despair.

Unfortunately for the truly bored preacher, his feelings are transmitted through all of his efforts to conceal them. The result is a skepticism on the part of the laity that the minister really lives in the world he recommends to others. Helmut Thielicke has said: "This is the point, it seems to me, where the secret distrust of Christian preaching is smoldering. Behind all the obvious and superficial criticism—such as that the sermon is boring, remote from life, irrelevant—there is, I am convinced, this ultimate reservation, namely, that the man who bores others must be boring himself. And the man who bores himself is not really living in what he—so boringly—hands out. 'Where your treasure is, there will your heart be also'—in this case the treasure of the heart seems not to be identical with what it is commending to others."[1]

This points us toward the true stance for the preaching minister. He must really live, as Christ did, in the real world. He must be a fully involved, fully knowledgeable, fully sympathetic inhabitant of his own time. If he cannot affirm his humanity in the time and place given to him, he will never minister to the human beings who do live there. No matter how much his love for Zion, he must also love his hometown. But if he is not also a citizen of the kingdom of God, if he cannot feel himself a part of the ongoing purposive movement of that kingdom in his own time, he will likewise never preach the redeeming word to a divided humanity.

This is a most solemn and profound realization. It challenges us to assert for ourselves a full participation in the divine Body as well as to confess of ourselves a completely human existence. We do not speak lightly when we speak of incarnational preaching, and that should be obvious at this point as at no other. We do not equate ourselves with Christ, nor challenge the unique authority of God, when we assert our participation in the divine Body. He has given this to us. We become the temple of the Spirit; Christ lives in us: "Nevertheless I live; yet not I, but Christ liveth in me" (Gal. 2:20).

Nevertheless, it is foolish, misguided theology to assert that Paul meant that my personality is unimportant, that God wants the death of my individuality, that in fact "I" am dead. The new life which is promised is for me. I am the person who is "born again." My own, my unique, my God-given self is made alive. I am no piece of dead equipment with the Holy Spirit sitting inside at the controls, pulling levers and moving my frame through its paces. What is dead is my alienation from God, from others, even from myself.

A man can attempt to use the Holy Spirit, however, for his own purposes. There is nothing more demonic than the preacher who chants the magic words of Scripture to cause the Spirit to do *his* bidding, all the while asserting, "The Spirit has never failed me. We must all *pay the price* to be empowered by the Spirit."

But the sin of Simon Magus was nothing more nor less than attempting to purchase the Spirit *for his own use* (Acts 8:18 ff.). The key to authentic ministry is not how much is wrought, but *what* is wrought, and *for whom,* and to *what end.* The earth had never seen more fervent evangelists than the Pharisees who journeyed endless miles without rest to gain a proselyte but whose converts were not children of God, but of hell.

The price of commitment paid by the preacher must always be for one purpose and one purpose only—that he might be a servant of God's will, and not of his own ambition. Samson "wist not that the Lord was departed from him" (Judg. 16:20) in his selfishness; but he was not the first, nor the last, servant of God to have that experience. George Buttrick has written, "The purity of a man's motives outweighs all other elements in his influence and almost completely cancels out other factors of difference."[2] The preacher's motivation can only be to point beyond himself to the Lord whom he serves. And only the preacher who has confessed his humanity is able to confess Christ.

After all, we must remember that Simon Peter himself, who made life's greatest confession—"Thou are the Christ"—had first already fallen upon his face and cried out, "Depart from me; for I am a sinful *man*, O Lord" (Luke 5:8). Only the preacher who has confessed that can confess him.

But what does it mean to be human?

Humanity and Personality

Listing character traits needed by the preacher is exactly as futile as listing the attributes of God, no matter how time-honored the practice. And for exactly the same reason. God cannot be described by any list of attributes, no matter how exhaustive the list. Nor can human personality. The traditional listings of personal characteristics needed by the minister generally become superficial and usually wind up sounding like the Boy Scout oath, "Brave, clean, and reverent."

At this point, an incarnational approach is again essential in understanding the preaching task. The humanity of the preacher is critical because he participates in the person of Christ. He does not understand the humanity of Christ because he understands himself; he understands what humanity means by looking at Jesus. The servant cannot be greater than his master. The preacher cannot be less human than his Lord. This is the great law for the personality of the preacher.

What does it mean for a preacher to be truly human?

1. First of all, no one needs to *become* human. He is already human. He simply needs to be *honest,* to avoid playing dishonest games with himself and others which deceive him into believing otherwise, and which retard or block entirely the process of becoming a maturing human. Spurgeon said:

There is such a thing as trying to be too much a minister, and becoming too little a man; though the more of a true man you are, the more truly will you be what a servant of the Lord should be. Schoolmasters and ministers have generally an appearance peculiarly their own; in the wrong sense, they are "not as other men are." They are too often speckled birds, looking as if they were not at home among the other inhabitants of the country, but awkward and peculiar. When I have seen a flamingo gravely stalking along, an owl blinking in the shade, or a stork demurely lost in thought, I have been irresistibly led to remember some of my dignified brethren of the teaching and preaching fraternity, who are so marvelously proper at all times that they are just a shade amusing. Their very respectable, stilted, dignified, important, self-restrained manner is easily acquired, but is it worth acquiring?[3]

Trying to be impressive is a great sin, and one that is easily self-excused. Do we not need to be "powerful" in our preaching? Do we not need to "impress" others with the gospel? Does not God use personality, our personality in that?

Yes, to all three questions. But that is the danger. The human element in proclamation is real, inescapable, important—and dangerous. P. T. Forsyth warned of the dangers of personality when he wrote: "No man has any right in the pulpit in virtue of his personality or manhood itself. . . . To be ready to accept any kind of message from a magnetic man is to lose the Gospel in mere impressionism. . . . And it is fatal to the authority either of the pulpit or of the Gospel. The church does not live by its preachers, but by its Word."[4]

Likewise, Bonhoeffer warned in strongest terms against developing a "cult of personality": "Every cult of personality that emphasizes the distinguished qualities, virtues, and talents of another person, even though these be of an altogether spiritual nature, is worldly and has no place in the Christian community; indeed, it poisons the Christian community."[5]

The grave danger is that we will not be servants of the Word, but of ourselves; that we will not invest our talents in his interests, but in ours; that we will not allow him to use us to preach his Word, but that we use him to project our words. Then if challenged, the dishonest preacher can always plead divine right and interpose God between himself and his people. Very convenient—and very dishonest.

2. After honesty, *naturalness* is the second requirement for true humanity. The preacher is indeed to "be himself." But what self? We are all so divided that it is usually a hollow claim to plead that "I was just being myself." What does it mean to "be yourself," to be "natural"?

Naturalness means not adding to or subtracting from your personality. It means being neither more nor less than you are. Some men try to be more than they are; they want to appear holier, or more profound, or more dynamic. Others are scared to death to seem to be as much as they are; they do not want to be regarded as zealous or devout. Both project a false, unnatural personality.

But how do I know *what* my natural personality is? We are all plagued by the ambiguity of selfhood.

Perhaps Bonhoeffer provided the best clue when he said, "In the service of Jesus I become natural."[6] Only the New Man in Christ is truly natural. The only self that is appropriate is *that* new man. This means that I do not need to imitate anyone else, neither do I need to imitate the Ideal Minister.

Imitation is not only the sincerest form of flattery, it is also the sincerest form of insecurity. No one is completely free of imitation, and modeling is a healthy and essential step in the maturing process of any minister. A preacher is lucky if the model he has chosen is a good one. Paul urged his followers to be imitators of him even as he was an imitator of Christ (1 Cor. 11:1).

But there is still a real danger in imitation. When a preacher continually apes the preaching manner of another, he is betraying a lack of personal security and identity. The natural desire for acceptance can lead to the unnatural imitation of others. Beyond the beginning stages of ministry, this practice indicates a warped concept of ministry and an unhealthy striving for prestige.

Many ministers preach with anything but the natural personality which is theirs. Either they speak with the personality of some preacher they admire (which is bad, but least worst), or more horribly, they adopt the collective personality which they imagine a preacher should have. Mary Shelley wrote about a similar attempt. Dr. Frankenstein pieced together the parts from a number of cadavers to make a man, but instead he created a monster. But no more so than the preacher whose personality is a composite of the bits and pieces of others, some long dead and nearly decomposed. And then when that monster roars and stalks about, he should not be surprised when children will not play about his feet.

3. The preacher will struggle all of his life with the inevitable tension between ego and humility, but true *humility* is another essential to true humanity. The answer certainly does not lie in unbridled self-assertion, but it is also most definitely not to be found in a Publicanish pride, a kind of "of course I am less than nothing," inverted pride, either. That is only a subtle way to force humility to serve pride.

Nor can humility be taken care of by semantic dodges. For example, saying "we" when he means "I" cannot cloak a preacher's outsized ego. The preacher who is always saying such things as "We are humbled by this opportunity to stand before you this morning . . .", or "We are grateful that you have listened to our words . . ." sounds like a speech choir. There is nothing humble about becoming a committee instead of an individual. Mark Twain once said that only three people were entitled to use the editorial "we": an editor, God, and a man with a tapeworm. Perhaps the "we" preacher does not consider himself either editorial or divine—he may be merely revealing his parasitic problem.

C. S. Lewis said that the truly humble individual will not be a greasy, "smarmy" kind of person who is always telling you that of course he is nobody; but if anything, he will strike you as a cheerful, intelligent person who enjoys life, and who takes a real interest in what *you* say to *him*. Being humble has nothing to do with believing yourself to be worthless. Only an incredibly obtuse preacher could fail to know his own obvious talents. Ministerial humility simply means recognizing the source of these gifts and firmly committing them to the service of Christ.

The theme of humility is a frequent one in Christian theology and has an ancient tradition. Chrysostom said in his homilies on Acts that some preachers lived for applause: "If they get applause from the multitude, it is to them as if they gained the very kingdom of heaven, but if silence follows the close of their speech, it is worse than hell itself, the dejection that falls upon their spirits from the silence." He himself had to forbid all applause from his audience—and this announcement itself brought the house down with applause![7]

When Henry Parry Liddon was about to deliver his first sermon at St. Paul's Cathedral, he wrote in his diary on the evening before, April 18, 1863; "Feel very unequal to preaching at St. Paul's tomorrow, both spiritually and physically. O Lord Jesus, help me—a poor sinner."[8] Similarly, D. T. Niles said of himself: "That is what I am. I am a sinner for whom Jesus died. I am just one of those who has been loved of God in Jesus at the cross. That is the central truth about me. All the rest is peripheral."[9] And Karl Barth has written, "We are *worthy* of being believed only as we are aware of our unworthiness. There is no such thing as *convincing* utterance about God except as Christian preaching feels its *need* . . ."[10]

4. When the Christian preacher is able to admit his own needs, he can stop feeling guilty about needing rest. This is another essential in true humanity—being human means *being able to rest*. Gods do not need rest; humans do. And no one needs to be rested more, in spirit and mind and body, than God's preachers. When we understand our part in ministry—which is not attempting to manage the whole world, but letting God be God—we can rest, physically and psychologically.

Compulsive recreation is not rest. Play is involved in rest, but without an understanding of our humanity, rest is impossible. We are never at ease, never at rest. But when God is God and I am his servant—hopefully a hard-working and faithful one, but still only a servant—I can be at ease. He is Lord: "The earth is the Lord's, and the fulness thereof; the world, and they that dwell therein" (Ps. 24:1). When the preacher really knows that, he can be at rest with the peace that is not understood. At work he can be at ease, and at rest he can be set free to play.

5. Being human also means *allowing others to be persons*. Some men who would stoutly insist on their own humanity are chronically unwilling to let anyone else be persons. "Don't preach at me" is a common, unfunny idiom. What it means is, "Don't overturn my personality! Who are you to be playing God? I am a person, and so are you."

Many preachers who would never recognize themselves as god-players nevertheless want to call all the shots and make all the decisions for every living creature. They are master of the house, the dog, and the church, and there is not much difference in the way they speak to each. Allowing others to be persons means respecting the uniqueness of their selfhood. It means never using approaches in preaching that are inappropriate for communication with other persons, approaches that are dictatorial or imperious, artificially sincere or seductive.

Letting God be God also means letting persons be persons. And the most miserable human being alive is the preacher who cannot be God and will not be a person.

6. As a matter of fact, preaching that really matters to people

does not result from high-handed techniques, but from caring. *True humanity means caring.* A great deal has been written about caring, so much that unfortunately "caring" has virtually become another fad word. The preacher who tries to mentally psych himself into deeply "caring" about his subject in order to be more persuasive is in trouble. Nothing is worse than the pose of phony concern. No one can care equally about all subjects, or doctrines, or even texts. Our caring about subjects varies with our interests. Anyone who attempts to appear equally passionate about every sermon subject destroys both perspective and credibility at the same time.

But if the preacher has been honestly apprehended by the word of God so that he ultimately cares about it; and if, at the most foundational levels of his being, that apprehension has led to its corollary, that he has been enabled to care about people, his concern cannot be concealed.

In short, you cannot develop concern from external enthusiasm for your subject. Caring about people, and the word which God has spoken and will speak for them, results in honest caring. Where a man's treasure is, his caring will be observed close by.

7. This kind of concern can only come from genuine involvement in the lives of the people to whom we minister. Paul Sherer has said, "You may begin your career with a doctrinaire interest in theology or in preaching as one of the fine arts. But pray God you may find yourself, little by little, drawn to human lives and human hopes and human fears."[11] If men suspect that we do not care, they will not listen—and properly so. Brand Blanshard writes, "But how often writers on religion, morals, or art leave one with the bleak impression that they have never come within miles of what these experiences are like to the people who have them!"[12] *Involvement with reality* is the final mark of true humanity.

Of course no one could experience all of life—just as no one could grasp all of the Scripture—but that is not the point. If the preacher seems not to understand either the real life of real people or the word of God for that existence, he is disqualified from proclamation of the gospel. But if he has known suffering, happiness, frustration, satisfaction—of whatever sort—and if he can bring the word of God to bear on these and other real conditions of human existence, he will be heard, and heard gladly. "The secret of reality in preaching is intelligibility, and the secret of intelligibility is interest. 'Interest,' 'interesting,' are to be understood in their etymological sense—*inter est*— that which is common to the speaker and hearer, that which they have between them."[13] When the preacher speaks of those things that he and his people have in common, interest always results.

To develop this mutuality of interest, the preacher needs sympathy—he must "feel with" others. The classic remark on this subject was that of John Broadus: "If I were asked what is the first thing in effective preaching, I should say sympathy; and what is the second thing, I should say sympathy; and what is the third thing, I should say sympathy."[14] No one could have preached with the aliveness of Jesus unless he also had his sympathetic interest in the human situation. Children and the common people heard him gladly because he welcomed little children and dined with publicans and sinners.

The first step—and a big one—toward increasing interest in preaching, and curing obscurity in language as well, is a reinvolvement in the common experiences of people as well as a renewed study of the living word. No one ever has a language problem alone. A context problem is invariably present. What a man is becomes language. If he is out of phase with his context, himself, and the word of God, his language will reflect his confusion. Insecurity, anxiety, striving for prestige, anger, fear, inability to relate to others, and unwillingness to obey God, all result in language failure. Brand Blanshard strikes it correctly: "Persistently obscure writers will usually be found to be defective human beings."[15] Tampering with vocabulary won't help that. The cure is far more radical. God must make a man right within his own skin. Then his language will make sense.

In summary, then, only a thoroughgoing commitment to the Bible as the word of God makes the present truly real, and only a thoroughgoing commitment to the present makes the message of the Bible fully intelligible. When the preacher positionizes himself at midpoint between his contemporary given and the historical given of the Gospel, he will find—perhaps to his surprise—that he is completely immersed in both. Perhaps even more surprisingly, he will find, as the early disciples did, that his human involvement enables his testimony to the divine Word.

5

CREDIBILITY AND CHARISMA

As we have seen, it was characteristic of the early disciples to refuse to play God. Paul's concern for the present and his commitment to the revealed Word refused to allow him to shift the focus from God to himself. By doing so, he gained a hearing for the gospel and established his own credibility at the same time.

In his day, just the reverse seemed to be true—as it always does. Halford Luccock has pointed out that Paul and Nero pursued opposite courses, and at that time Nero seemed to be right and Paul wrong. The contrast between the two is a fascinating study in credibility. Nero claimed divinity for himself, and Paul refused to do so when he had the chance. In that age Nero certainly appeared to have the last word. Yet no one would argue that Paul's credibility since that time hasn't been considerably better than Nero's, and Luccock reminds us that today men name their sons Paul, and their dogs Nero.

There is a profound lesson here for the preacher who will listen. "The one who will be greatest, let him be servant of all" (Mark 10:44). This truth applies also to preaching. The great sermon is the servant sermon. If the preacher would preach a great sermon, let him preach one that serves. Christ understood human ego drive and did not deny it. But he showed it the proper channel. When we lose our lives for his sake, and the sake of the Gospel, we find it. But the preacher who seeks to elevate himself for the sake of his own life loses everything.

Nor do we speak parabolically in saying this, but factually and practically. As we will see, credibility and charisma are both involved in this principle which Christ established for his servants. What is this element of credibility which Paul had and Nero lacked? Can it be analyzed?[1]

To understand this important concept, several terms need definition. *Credibility* may be defined as the weight given to the assertions of a speaker and the acceptance accorded them by his hearers. It is composed of two factors, trustworthiness and expertness. That is, the greater the trustworthiness and expertness of the speaker, the greater his credibility. *Expertness* is the extent to which a communicator is perceived to be capable of being a source of valid assertions; *trustworthiness* is the degree of confidence which the listeners have in the intent of the speaker to communicate valid assertions.

Credibility is highly important in communication: The listener's acceptance of the message of a high credibility communicator can be as much as four times greater than that of a low credibility communicator, one who is perceived as seriously lacking in trustworthiness and expertness. The credibility of any communicator is not static, however, but varies from situation to situation.

In the first place, no one is perceived as equally expert in all situations. A Supreme Court justice would usually be regarded as more expert than a plumber, but again, that all depends on whether a legal case is involved or a sink. Trustworthiness is generally a more stable factor in credibility than expertness, but not invariably so; it may also vary with the situation or the group.

The importance of these credibility factors for the minister is obvious. Unless he is perceived as both trustworthy and expert by the people with whom he ministers, his influence will be seriously impaired. He cannot hope to communicate the gospel with any degree of credibility if he is neither trustworthy nor expert. Obviously no one is completely expert on all questions—even within his own field of competence—and no one is perceived as equally trustworthy by all individuals. But the degree to which his listeners regard him as a person whose assertions are accurate and dependable will largely influence the degree of acceptance his message will gain.

A key word in this issue is *perceived*. Unfortunately, what a person actually knows, or how trustworthy he really is, is not always as significant as how expert or trustworthy he is perceived to be. Many knowledgeable, trustworthy preachers are not regarded with the esteem that they deserve, while some completely unscrupulous, ignorant preachers enjoy a reputation as real authorities of great character.

This means that credibility can be counterfeit and spurious. Many ministers suffer extreme anguish watching unscrupulous preachers glorying in undeserved adulation from people who have been duped through various deceitful and manipulative tricks which the preachers have used to appear expert and trustworthy.

But this should not prevent an ethical minister from examining his own expertness or trustworthiness, or the degree to which his congregation *perceives* him as such, in order to assess correctly his credibility in the community. Knowing about credibility factors, just as knowing about other elements in communication theory, does not imply unethical interests. On the contrary, it may mean removing obstacles that are causing the preacher to be a stumbling block in the communication of the gospel; or it may help him to eliminate the actual lack of expertness or trustworthiness which he discovers.

What do *expertness* and *trustworthiness* mean in the context of preaching? How can a minister be expert? What influences his congregation's perception of him as trustworthy?

Although no complete distinction is possible, expertness and trustworthiness roughly correspond in incarnational preaching with human existence and participation in the divine. *Expertness* means that as a human being, living among these people in this time and in this place, I must know something. I must understand the culture in which I live and the living needs of the people to whom I minister; and I must know how to interpret the word of God which speaks to them. This is my "expertness" as a preacher of the gospel.

But through the giving of myself to this task, which can only follow the giving of myself to Christ in his service, I become *trustworthy* and believable: "They which live should not henceforth live unto themselves, . . ." (2 Cor. 5:15). Obviously no one is completely selfless, just as no one is completely informed, but to the degree that we "lose our lives for his sake," to that degree we allow the Word to become incarnate in our preached words.

Let us examine the implications of this stance for the expertness and trustworthiness of the preacher of the Word.

Expertness

An expert in the pulpit is not an all-knowing, infallible source of information on all subjects in heaven and earth. If he tries to pretend that he is, the preacher's lack of expertness will be soon discovered and his trustworthiness will drop accordingly. As J. Edgar Park once put it, "An expert is an ordinary man far away from home, and a saint's reputation too often depends upon the silence of his family."[2]

Credibility is badly damaged by attempts to bluff his way on subjects where the preacher actually knows less than nothing. Expertness does involve information, of course, though that is not the only factor. The man who wants to have his message received must be sure of his facts, as sure as he can be, and where he is uninformed say so or keep quiet. No one expects him to know everything on all subjects anyhow, but people do expect him not to claim divine right on misinformation that causes even grade-school children in his congregation to giggle behind their hands.

Modern preachers who attribute the success of the long-antiquated "pulpit-princes" merely to their times would do well to be as informed as they were. It was said that when Spurgeon spoke of grouse-shooting you could be sure that he had read until he was expert on the subject, even if he made no more than a thirty-second reference to it. When Thomas Guthrie spoke on sailing, a man said, "He is an old sailor; at least, he was a while at sea!"; and when he spoke on medicine, someone said to another after the service, "If he *stick* [fail] the minister trade, the young man would make his bread as a surgeon!"[3]

Phillips Brooks fired a shot that is still hitting targets today: "In many respects an ignorant clergy, however pious it may be, is worse than none at all. The more an empty head glows and burns, the more hollow and thin and dry it grows."[4]

Expertness for the ministry, however, involves more than mere information. It also involves understanding: understanding of people, understanding of the situation in which people find themselves, and understanding of the relation of the biblical witness to both. No preacher will be perceived as expert, no matter how extensive his mental file cabinet on facts biblical or secular, unless he has a kind of *relational intelligence*; that is, unless he has gained significant insight from reflection on his experiences with other persons.

Some men display dazzling factual competence and unbelievable relational ignorance. They are unable to pick up obvious signals transmitted from individuals or audiences, and they misread and mishandle what few impulses they do get. They cannot anticipate reactions, they cannot understand feelings, they cannot deal meaningfully with human needs. Nathaniel Judson Burton said in his Yale Lectures, "They [the people] do not like to be fired at by a glib expert who knows guns perfectly but does not know men . . ."[5]

Increasing one's sensitivity to people is far more difficult than adding facts to one's brain. If a preacher realizes that his relational ability is low, he must work hard to listen more, and to read in areas where insight into personal factors can be improved. Perhaps he should also consider psychiatric consultation to gain insight into himself and his own life. Most preachers who lack insight into the needs of others themselves suffer badly from confused personal relations.

Other factors in expertness—age, leadership, and similarity of social background—are either largely out of the minister's control or else can be enormously improved by a demonstration of increased factual knowledge and improved human understanding.

Trustworthiness

If the minister cannot afford to be uninformed, he must be doubly certain of not being untrustworthy. An untrustworthy preacher of the word of God is unthinkable; and if people begin to think it, the credibility of the preacher is ruined. No amount of theological genius or biblical competence can save him.

Thielicke writes: "The fact is that a preacher is constantly betraying himself. When we meet a druggist, we do not necessarily note whether he loves or hates, whether he dispenses his pills with delight or whether he is eating his heart out in envy and care. . . . But with a preacher it soon comes out. . . . What the druggist thinks does not undermine the words with which he recommends this or that cough medicine but the preacher, by the state of his soul, can belie the words which have been committed to him, no matter how well chosen they are as he utters them."[6]

In other words, the personal traits of the preacher are far more involved in what he recommends than what the druggist dispenses. On the other hand, how would anyone react to a druggist who repeatedly pushed a cough remedy that he never used himself even though he owned stock in the company? His credibility would be exactly as low as the preacher who is manipulative for his own personal interests and inconsistent in his practice.

Let us examine briefly each of these three damaging elements in trustworthiness: *personal motivation, manipulative method,* and *inconsistent practice.*

Personal Motivation

A continuing liability to the preacher's credibility is his professional involvement in the Christian faith. Put bluntly, he is paid to advocate Christianity. For many people, this puts the sermon in the same category with a recommendation by an ad man for a product he is paid to promote. The laborer may be "worthy of his hire," but being hired doesn't help his credibility any.

The only chance for the paid Christian minister to maintain high credibility is to understand the difference between the "hireling" and the faithful servant.

The hireling runs away from the needs of the flock because he is a hireling; that is, because he is in it strictly for himself and what he can get out of it. The faithful servant is also paid— but he cares about his duties, and he loves the flock, and *he risks himself for them*. At that point he has nothing to gain for himself. He will not earn a penny more for the risk he takes or the extra pressure he subjects himself to. But he is faithful— trustworthy in the highest degree—because he is perceived as genuinely caring about his flock. "The good shepherd gives his life for the sheep" (John 10:11). It is not carrying things too far to say that the unequaled, centuries-long credibility of Jesus of Nazareth, even among non-Christians, is due to the completely selfless concern for others manifested in his life.

The preacher must be committed to the same selfless service as his Lord. If he is perceived as pursuing a ministry for gain, either monetary or professional; if he seems to care for nothing more than ladder-climbing and status-seeking; if he says only that which will please the galleries; if he prays loudly for "results" to build his reputation (and repeatedly insisting that "I just give God the glory" doesn't make it so)—then he may be assured, whatever his own inflated self-image, that his credibility is undermined by his obvious personal interests.

Manipulative Methods

Persuasion is not manipulation. Persuasion is the attempt to influence others. Everyone in the Bible who ever attempted to accomplish the will of God, whether Abraham or Moses or the prophets or Paul or Jesus, was involved in persuasion. Persuasion is not morally wrong, nor is it morally right. The question is *what* someone is being persuaded to do, and *why*, and *how*.

Persuading a distraught woman not to leap to her death from an office building is good; persuading a child to try heroin is evil. In these cases, *what* is being urged is the key factor. *Why* something is being urged is also vital to the ethical appropriateness of persuasion. To attempt to persuade a businessman that the Christian church can be deeply meaningful to his life and the life of his family is good; but to attempt to persuade him to affiliate with the church in order to get him to lower his price on property the church needs, is evil. *How* persuasion is done is likewise crucial. Persuasion that honestly and openly states all of the facts in a nonprejudicial way is fair and ethical, but persuasion that conceals or misrepresents facts is manipulative.

Manipulation, then, *may be defined as persuasion which is deliberately not in the best interest of the individual involved but is deceptively intended for the advantage of the persuader; or which attempts to get someone to do something he would not do if he had the facts.*

If the preacher cares about the commission of Christ to "go into all the world and make disciples," it will be impossible for him to avoid involvement in persuasive communication. But he should never resort to manipulation. His motivation and methods should always be closely and repeatedly examined, and if in doubt, he should find out how his persuasive attempts are perceived by others.

When an audience suspects that the preacher has something personal to gain from his persuasive efforts—more money, a larger pulpit, denominational status, popular acclaim—he is regarded as a manipulator. However, even if the end which the preacher seeks is good, he is still a manipulator if he uses deceitful means to accomplish it. For example, urging people to give money to carry out the work of the church might be a good thing both for the church and for the people, but promising that God will make them rich for so doing is manipulative. Such *specious promises* are often involved in religious manipulation.

Manipulation also is involved in *deliberately omitting significant facts* from an argument. A church might well need a new building, but failing to mention that interest rates are at a ten-year high could be a damaging blow to the credibility of the argument. In such cases, potentially damaging facts should be discussed openly and dealt with. Then if the need is great enough to override them, persuasion has been accomplished without manipulation. If not, it is better to discover the problem sooner than later. Churches who later learn that they were manipulated by their pastor generally have rather severe reactions toward him. In fact, he may be persuaded (or manipulated) into going elsewhere.

One of the most unforgivable forms of manipulation is preaching a "cheap grace"—omitting the full demands of discipleship—to lure people into the membership of the church. Usually this hucksterism combines an oversimplified sales pitch with false promises of a carefree, God-will-give-you-whatever-you-want life. This kind of Mohammedan sermon will promise anything to get "joiners" so that the "evangelist" can put another notch in his Bible (and these statistics, of course, he will modestly include in his next brochure).

Once people have been manipulated like that, they present a continuing problem for the church. If they do not drop out altogether in disillusionment, they frequently perpetuate the shallow, manipulative methods that attracted them in the first place.

Inconsistency

Many preachers suffer from low trustworthiness because they are simple careless and inconsistent in their remarks. They are not deliberately manipulative, nor are they self-centered, but they are careless with facts. They express too many opinions on subjects where they are poorly informed. They cite half-remembered facts on the spur of the moment and someone catches them in an inaccurate statement.

Everyone makes this mistake at times, of course, frequently without ever realizing it. But if this kind of inaccuracy persists, the preacher is quickly labeled as uninformed, careless, and untrustworthy.

Sermon illustrations are a notorious field for inaccuracy and inconsistency. The expression, "preacher stories" has become idiomatic for unbelievable assertions which are fanciful at best and downright dishonest at worst. Every illustration should be factually correct and carefully checked for accuracy. One unscientific science reference, or one nonhistorical historical reference, can seriously damage a preacher's credibility.

The primary issue at stake in trustworthiness, however, is usually not so much *factually incorrect* remarks as *exaggerated or untrue remarks;* such as illustrations which never happened at all or which were told as if they happened to the speaker, when in fact they did not. Some laymen have heard several pastors in different churches tell of having the same identical experience.

Two Protestant bishops (who obviously had just returned from the same conference) began their chapel addresses at a university with the same story, an incident which supposedly had happened to each of them the Sunday before as they greeted people on their way out of church. The second bishop, no more dishonest than the first, was hooted into silence, and his embarrassed host had to stand and explain to him the reason for the outburst. He never recovered, and the Christian cause almost didn't recover on that campus either.

If pastors were hooted down every time they were discovered in an untrue, exaggerated, or wildly inaccurate remark, we would have shorter sermons and more interesting worship services.

If a story sounds unbelievable—even if you personally trust the source of it—either be able to document it or don't tell it. No story is worth the loss of a congregation's trust, no matter how dramatic and appealing it may be.

Consider, for example, this story. It was Napoleon's genius to ignite the common man to fervid patriotism. To exemplify the French spirit, he used to tell this one:

Once he came upon an old soldier who had one arm and still wore his uniform, on which was displayed the Legion of Honor.

"Where did you lose your arm?" the emperor asked.

"At Austerlitz, sire," the soldier replied.

"And for that you were decorated?"

"Yes, sire. It is a small token to pay for the Legion of Honor."

"It seems to me," Napoleon said, "that you are the kind of man who regrets he didn't lose both arms for his country."

"What then might be my reward?" asked the old soldier.

"Oh, in that case I would have awarded you a double Legion of Honor."

With that, the old soldier drew his sword and immediately cut off his other arm.

For years the story circulated and was accepted without question until one day someone asked, "How?"

Trustworthiness, perhaps more than any other characteristic, is expected of the preacher of the gospel. A congregation may be willing to forgive a lack of expertness, but if they perceive their preacher as untrustworthy, his credibility is destroyed. And no one in society should have greater credibility than the man who speaks for Christ.

Charisma: Not the Coin-in-the-fish's-mouth of Preaching

Closely related to credibility, and yet distinct from it, is the question of charisma. What is this mysterious element? Is it capable of analysis? If so, what significance, if any, does the concept have for the Christian preacher?

In communication theory, charisma has most often been associated with political leadership. Some public figures have been regarded as possessing mystical, almost magical powers of leadership and persuasion. Such persons are said to be charismatic, possessed of gifts which defy analysis. (The concept is closely related to Christian sources; in fact, the term, "charismatic leadership," itself was borrowed by Max Weber from Rudolf Sohm's history of the church.[7]

Charisma is neither intrinsically good or bad. Some leaders have used their charisma for good, others for evil: Winston Churchill, Franklin Roosevelt, John F. Kennedy, Adolph Hitler, Gandhi, and Mao Tse-Tung, among others, are widely regarded as charismatic figures.

Christianity is also fertile soil for charisma. Only politics can rival the church as a producer of charismatic leaders. A number of Christian preachers are particularly remembered as charismatic figures, among them Chrysostom, Francis of Assisi,

Savonarola, Martin Luther, John Knox, William Booth, Studdert Kennedy, Martin Luther King, Fulton J. Sheen, and Billy
Graham. Obviously this group is also a mixed bag of gifts,
attitudes, and ministries. Is there anything in common among
these people? Can charisma be attained? Or is it a pure gift, like
one's height or the color of his eyes? Is charisma the coin-in-
the-fish's mouth of preaching, something miraculously caught?

Until quite recently, only a very few serious studies, such as
those of Max Weber in political science, have dealt with charisma. Many authorities on communication theory still continue
to consider charisma as the result of a complex combination of
many credibility factors or perhaps the possession of one of
these to an extraordinary degree. One author of an excellent
work on persuasive communication says of charismatic figures,
"They remain as individuals whose effect on audiences and
history is not explained by research literature."[8]

Continuing research, however, has begun to narrow the
search for the key to charisma. Two basic characteristics seem
to typify the charismatic relationship: first, *charismatic leaders
are perceived as possessed by a purpose which is greater than
themselves;* and second, *charismatic leadership requires a
charismatic community.*

All of the charismatic leaders previously named definitely
have one characteristic in common: They all were perceived as
having given themselves in utter selflessness to a cause greater
than themselves. People flocked to these leaders because they
were able to project this sense of complete abandonment to the
greater interest. In the case of Churchill, it was the defense of
Britain; in the case of Hitler, it was the establishment of the
Third Reich. But people gave fanatical allegiance to both
because they believed these leaders to be totally dedicated to
the common good rather than to personal interests. They may
have been, or they may not have been. The essential fact is that
they were perceived as absolutely absorbed in a cause greater
than themselves.[9]

This means that unscrupulous politicians, or preachers, can
counterfeit commitment and fraudulently lead. They may care

nothing for a cause or for the people who fanatically follow them. They may care only for money, or power, or status. They may not be selfless at all but selfish, vain, and arrogant. Their only cause may be success, and the only people they care about may be themselves. But because they project the image of a selfless leader who has given up all personal ambition to serve the Great Cause, they are believed and followed.

Second, charismatic leadership requires a charismatic community. A definitive characteristic of the charismatic relationship is the "unqualified belief in the man and his mission" by a group of followers.[10] That is, the purpose which he projects must match the burning desire of a people. Francis of Assisi made himself poor for Italy's poor; Gandhi starved himself for India's starving. Unless the purpose of the leader matches that of his community, or unless he can arouse the people to his goals, he will have no charisma at all.

This means that no leader is perceived as charismatic by all communities. The same people who regarded John F. Kennedy as a magnetic leader would not feel the same about Adolf Hitler, nor was Martin Luther King charismatic for most members of the white community in the South. These leaders represented the dreams of the purposive communities which followed them.

These are the two basic characteristics of the charismatic relationship, but *what are the personal traits* of the charismatic leader? At least eight such characteristics have been identified as common to charismatic figures: (1) exposure to varied environments and norms; (2) the ability to identify with, have empathy toward, and communicate with the plurality within the group they serve; (3) a high energy level, or an extraordinary degree of vitality; (4) presence of mind or composure under conditions of stress or challenge; (5) unswerving dedication toward their goals; (6) the ability to project the impression of a powerful mind and range of knowledge; (7) a capacity for innovation and originality; (8) identification with the continuity of tradition, and the proclamation of the vision of a new and different order to come.[11]

There are many fascinating implications from this study for the Christian church and its preaching. To begin with, reread this list with Jesus of Nazareth in mind. It could scarcely describe him better. And if that is so, *this means that the follower of Christ, the one who is to be Christlike, will also be possessed of certain charismatic characteristics.* Even briefly touching on a few of these traits will suggest intriguing possibilities.

In the first place, if exposure to varied norms is an important experience for the charismatic leader, then our pluralistic age is not the detriment to charismatic leadership it is usually believed to be. Jesus lived in just such an age. And who should have more empathy toward this plurality—rich and poor, educated and uneducated, multiracial—than the Christian? Jesus could identify with these people and communicate with them. His disciples should be able to do the same. Likewise, the enthusiasm for life, the composure under stress, the dedication to goals, the understanding and innovation that typified Christ, should also typify those he has claimed.

Perhaps most significant, the preacher of the historic faith should be able to identify with the continuity of tradition, as did his Lord, but he must also proclaim the vision of a new and different order to come, as Jesus did. It is also interesting for the role of preaching that "the proclamation of his [the charismatic leader's] goal or mission may play no small part in initially generating the charismatic relationship."[12]

The very fact that charismatic traits can be identified means that charisma cannot be written off as magic. It is not absolutely mysterious, no matter how complex it is or how difficult to analyze in detail. It is not inherited. Some people may seem to be born with it, while others appear incapable of ever possessing it to the slightest degree. *But these are the exceptions.* If a person has minimal abilities in the areas described, and more important, if he can give himself to a cause worthy of his complete abandon and can project his feelings to a community of corresponding concern, he will be perceived as charismatic.

Few people may ever achieve the charisma of a Luther or a

Gandhi or a Churchill—for one thing, few will stand at the intersection of time and need as they did, nor will many possess their extraordinary communicative talents—but charisma is relative, and the gift of extraordinary leadership is not limited to a few charismatic geniuses.

Can the average preacher be charismatic? He can be, and to some extent, he should be. Who should be more entitled to completely abandon himself to a great cause than the minister of the gospel? Who, in more honesty, and with more integrity, should be better able to project this concern to people? Who should be be more justified in urging a community to join him in a common cause? Where should anyone expect to find a readier matching community of concern, a truly charismatic community, than in the Christian church?

If the church seems lacking in charismatic leadership, the blame must be shared. Perhaps it is true that its preachers have not been able to completely lose themselves in the Christian cause, or perhaps they have been timid and hesitant to project to others their genuine commitment to that cause. But perhaps it is also true that they have not found their concern matched by a corresponding charismatic community. Unless the church is equally committed to the common cause of Christ, unless the church is willing to lose itself for the sake of the world, and unless the church encourages its leaders by its equal devotion, it need not altogether blame the ministry. *Periods of great charismatic leadership in the church have been matched by great charismatic communities.* One encourages the other, and both are produced by obedience to the word of God.

Neither the church nor its preachers should seek after charisma. That would be self-serving and therefore utlimately self-defeating. "But seek ye first the kingdom of God, and his righteousness; and all these things shall be added unto you also" (Matt. 6:33).

6

IMPACT, COMMUNION, AND SHOCK

The study of credibility and charisma in the man who preaches corresponds closely with another issue, the question of impact in the message which he preaches. It is possible for the disciple of the twentieth century after Christ to communicate with the same impact that characterized the preaching of the apostles of the first century? How can he shape the sermon so that his words allow the Word to strike with the fresh impact which always typifies the gospel?

Before we can answer these questions, we must first understand the relationship between impact, communion, and shock. This understanding is not only vital to the act of preaching but to the larger service of worship, and indeed, even to the total ministry of the preacher himself. First, what is impact?

Put most simply, impact is the effect which a communication has upon its hearer. Translated for the preaching setting it means, Does my sermon make a difference? More specifically, What, if anything, happens to people because of my preaching that would not happen without it?

These questions immediately arouse emotions. Few preachers can reflect on them five seconds without experiencing a change in blood pressure. Some men immediately become angry, or at least annoyed. ("Annoyed" being what an angry preacher is when not alone.) This angry group is a curious mixture of left and right, theologically and homiletically.

Those on the right who see the preaching of the Word as an almost magical, or hypersacramental, and virtually objective reality, resent the idea that "I" or "my" sermons are involved at all. The preached word has impact. Period. Curiously, the left feels the same, but for totally different reasons. Who am I to think that I have the right to change anybody? Isn't this the manipulative method of the huckster? And since when is it my business to care about whether I am effective or not?

Other preachers just feel depressed, or a little sad, at these questions. They are fairly sure that their sermons aren't making any difference. They have become resigned to preaching because they are still obliged to, or because they have a dogged faith in preaching—if not in their preaching. For them, the answer to this question is simple: My preaching has no impact.

If preaching were a completely objective event, the preacher would not need to think about the possible impact, or lack of it, of his message. Impact would be guaranteed by the objective Word itself calling forth an irresistible response from its subjects.

But in order for that to be true, two things would have to change. First, the preacher's own involvement in the act of preaching would have to be overridden or abolished altogether; and second, the congregation's free human response would have to be destroyed and replaced by a programmed response to the message, a kind of divine posthypnotic suggestion. Since both of these conditions are obviously out of the question, the preacher cannot avoid the question of impact.

This is not to say that there cannot be an overemphasis on impact, on effect, on "results." There is an illegitimate concern involving impact. Whenever a preacher makes impact his primary concern, he is liable to all sorts of dangers. Even if he has scrupulously swept his homiletical house free of indifferent preaching, he has made it all the more habitable for demons if his only care is for impact. Manipulative methods and a gallery-pleasing mentality are sure to occupy his preaching. Then he has betrayed the gospel by lapsing into a false subjectivity, an overeagerness to impress, to please, to excite.

On the other hand, only a false objectivism can ignore impact. People do matter. They are real, and they are really there, and the preacher is really one of them. As a person he was called of God to preach; as persons with distinct needs and hearing handicaps, the congregation sits before him. The human element is no less important in preaching than the divine element. The dangers on the people-side of incarnational preaching cannot be overcome by denying the reality of the human element or ignoring it. You cannot make God more there by obliterating the humanity of the worshipers or their preacher.

With all of the dangers, then, that can result from a preoccupation with impact, nevertheless we cannot ignore it, the detriment of its absence or the power of its presence.

But just as the communication of the gospel stands at midpoint between the historical given and the existential given, so impact stands between communicative communion and communicative shock. In order to analyze impact correctly, we must begin with an understanding of communion as a function of communication; then we can observe the two factors which yield impact; and finally, we can see how an excess of these factors leads to communicative shock.

Communion

To the right of impact stands communion. Technically, its true name is *phatic communion*. Phatic communion is presymbolic language. "Hello" is an example. In fact, all "hello" language—such as greetings, comments about the weather, and generalized inquiries ("How are you?")—is presymbolic, or communal, language.

Such language is presymbolic because it does not actually represent anything concrete but only serves to acknowledge mutual existence. It says, I am here and you are there, and I recognize our mutuality. Otherwise, these expressions don't mean anything. "Hello" is simply the greeting-call of the

American human (an interesting specie); and "How are you?" is an empty inquiry that expects an equally empty reply— "Fine, thanks"—and one that is actually in mortal dread of anything more substantive.

As insignificant as these aimless niceties appear, they are really highly meaningful forms of communication. Phatic communion is an important language use because it creates bonds of understanding between people, and the small agreements which are reached lead to the possibility of larger agreements later. Even more significant, recognizing the existence of another person is the first step toward community with him, and ignoring his existence is a sure-fire way to destroy any possibility of it.

If you want to test this theorem, simply ask yourself how you feel about the person who "never speaks," or how you feel when someone passes you repeatedly and looks right through you as if you were not there. Even if the oversight is completely innocent, it is difficult not to develop feelings which later make true communication and friendship very difficult. A warm greeting and a genuine interest, however brief or passing, does exactly the opposite: You think, "That's a person I'd like to know better."

Many a preacher has suffered from an innocent oversight in this regard. As old sister McGillicudy likes to tell it, "The pastor drove *right by me* downtown today, and never even spoke!" (The fact that the pastor never spoke because he never even *saw* sister McGillicudy is beside the point.) He has committed an unpardonable sin—he ignored her existence.

Probably everyone knows Mrs. McGillicudy and doesn't pay too much attention to her consistently offended manner. But the pastor cannot afford for the same to be said by the Smiths and Joneses of his congregation, too, or he is in serious trouble. Then, "He doesn't care"—even if he does. Communion is important, however trivial it may seem (it usually doesn't appear trivial to *us*), and woe to him who ignores it.

This language exists because of a fact in human existence. Its reality can no more be ruled out of the universe by "getting above such trivia" than the law of gravity can be repealed by someone with superior scientific understanding. The arrogant scientist who steps off the twelve-story building will still hit the pavement, and the superior theological thinker who ignores the need of people for simple language communion will be dropped equally hard.

Greeting parishioners on the street, however, is not the only use of communicative communion for the minister. At least as significant is his use of the familiar and the common in his preaching.

Language communication is only made possible through the familiar. If "corpulent" is not in the listeners' vocabulary, then the speaker had better use "fat." The word may not be as delicate, but at least it's familiar—and therefore understandable. Likewise, you can read English, and likely not Arabic, because of your experience. (Unless, of course, you happen to be from Saudi Arabia, in which case, the reverse is true. But since you don't read English, my telling you so isn't of any use.) And because you and I have the English language in common, communication is possible.

The use of the familiar is also important to remind us of our common experience. The whole question of community, of oneness, of a sense of a "we-ness" and "us-ness" instead of a "you-ness" and "me-ness," is at stake. Without anything familiar, communication is literally impossible. Without something that is familiar, a sense of community is not possible.

There is a certain legitimacy for the longing on the part of the congregation for old hymns, familiar terms. These things establish identity with the common experience. They say, "We are a part of the same community." Without some of the familiar, at least, from a Christian's past worship experience, a sense of strangeness and even disorientation occurs.

That is why the young preacher is in serious trouble who goes out to his first rural pulpit and announces, "We aren't singing any more of those old hymns. I'm taking up the hymnals and passing out mimeographed sheets of meaningful hymns which my wife will play on the Sitar. And though I don't expect you to understand it, for the first few weeks I will

be sharing revolutionary insights with you from my advanced
theological training to bring us to a mutual understanding."
And they will likely come to one—the church will be looking
for another preacher, and he will be looking for another pulpit.

Of course he can console himself by telephoning his philosophical friends at long-distance and telling them that he has
just proved his fidelity to the Cause by getting asked to leave
his simple pulpit; but his friends—if better balanced—may
suspect that all he has proved is his own poor judgment and
perhaps his lack of Christian spirit. And he himself may
secretly nurture a deep hurt and confusion at his rejection,
which will likely grow into a bitter disillusionment with "what
can be done" with the church. He may think he has champi-
oned the cause of truth and progress when quite likely what he
has done is to refuse to say hello to the community, or even to
have slapped people in the face when they stuck out their
hands.

To those who insist, "But they aren't even *thinking* of the
words of those old hymns," the only reply is, you're right. They
aren't. But the cognitive value in hymn singing isn't the only
one. When the familiar notes are sounded and the familiar
words are sung, there is a sense of unity, of this is what we are,
this is what we've experienced, this is what we have in common. The same is true of familiar terms so long as they, as well
as the hymns, are not theologically illegitimate or untrue to the
Christian faith. Their age or familiarity alone cannot negate
their value or meaningfulness to the spirit of community.

And it is more than a trifle inconsistent that some who most
loudly insist on establishing true community are most offended
by the familiar. (Often their own unpleasant early religious
experiences are projected upon the attitudes of everyone else
toward the familiar.) Frequently, if not invariably, those new
and innovative methods, terms, hymns, or elements of worship
which are regarded as meaningful eventually become locked
into an invariable, repetitious pattern at least as predictable,
and ultimately as "meaningless"—except for the neocult, to
whom they speak of the familiar—as the older ways so vio-
lently rejected.

The question which should be ultimately determinative, of course, is not whether terms or methods are old or new, traditional or innovative, but whether they best communicate the whole message of the gospel to the whole man. Communicative communion can play a valuable part in that.

But it is at this very point that the danger arises in the use of language as communion. The communication of the gospel can be forgotten entirely in an effort to establish commonality with the audience. We have all sat through almost unbearable services where absolutely nothing happened at all except mutual back-slapping, endless "hello" saying, and vigorous head-nodding. If an idea walked into the room, it would be voted down. In these services the highest good is imagined to be a group sitting in a friendship circle, holding hands, smiling vacuously, and singing "Blest Be the Tie that Binds."

People may become very enthusiastic after one of these services in which nothing was said that they did not already know and had not already heard a thousand times, particulary if it was what they wanted to hear and if it was said more fervently than usual. "Wasn't that great!" But if asked what was so "great" about it, they may become somewhat confused and reply, "I don't know—but wasn't that the best you ever heard!" Oratory is born in this climate of striving to say nothing and to say it better than it has ever been said before.

It is this sort of perversion of true communion that causes people to become almost violent on the subject of the traditional. But cliché repeating and playing to the galleries, or "saying what they want to hear," is not honest communion in the Christian faith, but a base and often hypocritical pandering to the appetites of the crowd. Such "worship" soon becomes stereotyped and sterile.

In fact, about the only motivation produced by this consistent use of nonthink nonspeech is a fierce defensive rejection of anyone or anything that is different. The Bible may be quoted and the Holy Spirit may be invoked, but it is apparent that both are only used as familiar tools rather than heeded as dynamic challenges to an ongoing faith. Pharisaism of the lowest sort is only a step away, and the worst witch hunts and the most deadly cultic institutionalism alike have resulted from this language abuse.

Again, it is important to remember that no wing of the church has a monopoly on this kind of error. Normally, the "conservative" or right wing of the church is identified with traditional cliché language and cultic nonspeech. But the "liberal" or left wing of the church can be just as guilty. Whenever the gospel is forgotten in an effort to please, to conform to culture, to innovate for innovation's sake, a new language of Zion and deadening tradition is on the way. The innovative order of today soon becomes the expected routine of tomorrow, and the radically up-beat terminology which is so daring at first quickly sounds dated.

This aging process is inevitable, and really is not so bad—if the innovations actually communicated the meaning of the faith better in the first place—but the accompanying mentality of antitraditionalism is usually as fiercely defensive of its own set routine and cultic language as the most ardent traditionalism.

Nevertheless, in spite of these dangers inherent in communal language, it is obvious that community of whatever sort, traditional or innovative, demands a certain degree of the common and the familiar. This does not need to be engineered into a communication method. It will occur naturally, due to inherited or created tradition, unless prevented. On the other hand, excessive phatic communion leads to noncommunication and boredom because of an absence of impact.

The next question, therefore, involves impact. What are the factors which result in impact for communication? And how can these be developed without destroying true communion or causing communicative shock?

Impact

Impact is the produce of two forces, predictability and distance. Impact is in inverse proportion to both: the greater the predictability and distance of a communication, the less the impact.

1. *Predictability*. Impact is promoted by a lack of predictability. For example, if your little girl tells you that she is going to hide in the hall and whisper "Boo!" when you pass, it really isn't very scary and daddy has to work hard at looking frightened. But if not warned, that same simple act can make a normally unemotional two-hundred-pound man try to climb into the attic without benefit of stairs.

Much preaching lacks impact because of its absolute predictability. It begins the same; it ends the same. Its feeling level is the same; its volume level is the same. It is always flat, or it is always excited. Its order of arrangement is always the same, or nearly so. Its topics vary, but not much. Preachers change churches and churches change preachers in an effort to get some kind of variety into the preaching and worship experience.

Some preachers of integrity absolutely cannot understand why their messages have so little impact, while their laymen are frequently carried away (sometimes literally so) by another preacher or evangelist who is absolutely nothing but shallow and flamboyant. This kind of spiritual seven-year itch or religious middle-age crisis on the part of laymen may be regrettable, but it happens because impact in the church relationship has dropped to zero due to the utter boredom and absolute predictability of the experience.

The cure for the problem is not for the preacher to start telling death-bed stories or wearing loud suits, anymore than buying a new wig or changing lipstick shades can really do much about a wife's problems with a restless husband. Some slight external changes in presentation, manner, or style may be called for, and within the limits of a man's own personality may help some.

But the only real cure must take place at a deeper level. He must find within the Bible, within his congregation, within himself—within life itself—the authentic uniqueness of reality. Sameness plagues preaching, worship, and ministry when the incredible variety of life is blocked out and one facet of it is monotonously played and replayed.

The only predictability to which the preacher should be

committed is the same predictability which Jesus had, and that is a consistent devotion to the will of God. But since that devotion will involve him in ministry with all kinds of people in every imaginable setting in his ever-changing contemporary existence, as well as with the historical acts of God and the life of Christ in all of their incredible depth and richness, an authentic, unforced variety will be the inevitable result. As a matter of fact, boredom of minister and people is the surest sign of an inattention to the living Word in our midst and of a preoccupation with a few threadbare themes of our own.

In short, to increase impact, decrease predictability. Perhaps a simple varying of liturgy, or sermon approach, or some other external adjustment is all that is needed. Likely, however, authentic unpredictability cannot be created so easily from the surface of things. But listening to the whole message of the whole Bible and broadening his ministry with people will give the preacher the same refreshingly different approach to life which Jesus had.

2. *Distance*. The greater the distance in communication, the less the impact. Caesar had an often-quoted motto for his legions: "Shorten your swords and lengthen your boundaries." The same is true for communication: "Shorten the distance and increase your impact."

Sometimes actual spatial distance is a factor in impact. For example, if an airplane crashes in Bolivia, we scarcely notice the headlines—we should, but we usually don't. If one crashes in our backyard, however, we are not likely to stop talking about it for the rest of our lives.

It is not accidental that such powerful communicators as Spurgeon and Whitefield preferred to be surrounded by audiences. The actual physical distance between the speaker and his audience significantly affects impact. As much as is possible, the preacher should seek to be among the people as he speaks. Nothing worse ever happened to Christian proclamation than locating the pulpit at one end of long, bowling-alley shaped churches where at least 50 percent of the audience need opera glasses to see the platform.

Many of these problems cannot be overcome immediately,

however; and even if they were, another kind of distance is far more significant than physical distance—psychological distance.

Continuing our analogy, that same airliner that went down in Bolivia will attract higher interest if people from your hometown are on it. If you knew some of those people personally, the impact is greater still. And if your wife or family were among the passengers, your involvement would be acute. (Naturally if you yourself were on board, the impact would be absolute.) In each case, the physical distance remains the same, but the psychological distance is being progressively shortened.

All of us have had such experiences. Our own involvement with the people or the problem caused the distance to drop dramatically and the impact of the event to jump. While in Europe I caught fragments of a report of a bus wreck in New Mexico in which a number of people were killed. Later I learned it was a church bus loaded with young people going to a religious retreat sponsored by my denomination. Then I learned that the group was from a church where I had preached several times. Finally I was told that some people I knew had been among those killed. With each added personal involvement with the incident, the impact of the event upon me was radically heightened.

Preaching will lack impact unless the psychological distance between the message and the hearer is short. This means that the preacher must talk about things that matter to me. Unless I am involved with the issues at stake, the psychological distance between it and me will be too great and the impact of his message will be low.

That is why doctrinal preaching is generally regarded as the most difficult preaching—not just because the doctrines themselves are profound, but because they are usually presented as abstract theological concepts which could only matter to a professional theologian. Unless a doctrine matters to people—and when correctly understood, they all do—then what is the use of preaching about it?

As in the case of predictability, shortening psychological

distance does not call for artificial method adjustment. The preacher does not need to sit around craftily figuring the most personal, emotionally loaded subjects to fire at his congregation. What he *does* need to do is to really understand that "the sabbath was made for man, and not man for the sabbath" (Mark 2:27)—or in other words, that the words and ways of God were designed for *people*, for living, breathing, very human people, and not for themselves.

When the preacher recognizes the genuine human involvement in every line of Scripture, and when he realizes that what people care about and need, at the deepest level of reality, is what the Bible talks about, then his preaching will bridge the psychological distance between the historical word and the contemporary world.

But when the predictability of the church is absolute and the distance between itself and people is infinite, is it any wonder that its impact is *null*? The words and deeds of Christ struck the world with incredible impact because their genuineness was so unpredictable and their involvement with life was so intimate. Any preacher who has the faith to become involved with the incarnate life of Christ in his own ministry—to whatever degree, even that of a grain of mustard seed—will see the impact of his proclamation increase.

Shock

To the right of impact stands communion; to its left stands shock. Too much predictability and too much distance cause a message to have zero impact; but too little predictability at point-blank range can lead to communicative shock. And when hearers go into communicative shock, the death of communication is not far away.

Shock in communication means that the level of impact has been raised to intolerable levels. The listener drops a barrier between himself and the speaker to prevent further communication. Hearing is no longer possible. The message itself is lost because its impact stunned rather than motivated. Impact is not an absolute good, of which there can never be too much. If impact becomes the goal of preaching, rather than the communication of the gospel, positive harm can be done.

In order to understand the effect of communicative shock, let us examine another example. Physical shock can be caused either by physical impact or by psychological impact: A teenage boy went into shock and died after being struck in the chest by a rock thrown by a lawnmower; when told at the hospital of his death, the boy's mother also collapsed in shock. In both cases, impact was the cause of shock.

When we are *shocked*, in the psychological meaning of the word, it is always because we are surprised, startled, impacted by the unexpected. A certain distance factor is at work, too, because we must be close to an event, either spatially or psychologically, before we can care enough to be shocked.

If this factor is projected into communication, it is not difficult to understand how communicative shock can ensue. Whenever a sermon—or for that matter, a worship service—becomes so different and unpredictable in its content or style that it is almost disorienting to the congregation, shock may result. Or, if that which is dealt with in the sermon is so threatening and personally unendurable to the hearer that escape is the only alternative, then distance has been reduced to the point that communicative shock is inevitable.

Obviously a delicate balance must be maintained between saying things so predictably and remotely that utter boredom results, and shocking people so severely with the unpredictable and the threatening that hearing is blocked or even killed. If the expectations of an audience for a sermon or a service are too badly frustrated, they may be disoriented and the message itself lost; on the other hand, if their expectations are too closely met, they may be left satisfied but unchallenged.

Again, the key to maintaining this balance is the focus of the message. What is its purpose? To startle, to shock, to innovate for the sake of novelty? Or to awaken complacency to the challenge of the gospel, to speak plainly that which must be heard, and more than heard—accepted and acted upon?

But "speaking plainly" is not as easy as it sounds. What we mean by a word-symbol may not be what the listener hears. Understanding the *principle of contiguity* can help us at this point. That is, the nearest meaning for a word or symbol in the mind of the listener is the one that will be heard rather than a more distant one. As we will see, this has important implications for the question of shock.

For example, if a preacher uses the word *myth* in the usual context, his listeners are more likely to take the word in its Greek setting than in a theological one. He may not intend in the slightest to convey the fanciful imagery of the Greek legends, but since that is the nearest-lying meaning for *myth* in their minds, they will decode the word in that sense. Even if redefined, the connotative and emotive influences of the previous meaning may hang on to make the word suspect in spite of all efforts to the contrary.

The same holds true for symbols. In some circles the wearing of a robe by the preacher would convey a negative impression, while in others the absence of one would do the same thing. In both cases, the near-lying meaning for clerical garb in the minds of the congregation dominates whatever the minister wished to convey otherwise.

Contiguity cannot be ignored in communication. When it is, shock usually follows. No one could be expected to know all of the near-lying meanings for words and symbols in the minds of the congregation—in fact, these meanings vary from person to person—but deliberately ignoring conventional meanings for more esoteric ones is a tricky business in communication. If the preacher wants to try, he should at least know what he is doing. Then if he decides the meaning transfer is worth the risk, he can make the effort more intelligently.

But word-redemption, for word-redemption's sake, is of dubious value. It is questionable whether some terms are worth redeeming, or whether they carry such an emotive load that the effort is questionable anyhow.

Obviously someone will always be going into communicative shock over something unfamiliar or distressing—in fact, psuedoshock is a favorite Pharisaic hobby—and the preacher cannot become verbally paralyzed in a hopeless effort to avoid the complaints of hypocrites, radicals, and cranks. But neither is he entitled to deliberately shock sincerely honest Christians in order to appear more theologically literate than they. It is true that he has been called to a redemptive ministry—but for persons, not for favorite terms.

Sometimes radical innovation and shocking content in preaching and worship are nothing more than a desire on the part of the preacher to punish, to strike back, sometimes at people long dead or times long gone. If so, he should not be surprised when people strike back or refuse to allow him to work out his problems on them, nor should he deceive himself that he is a martyr for the truth.

The progress of the kingdom has likely been as often hindered by meaningless innovation as by meaningless tradition. "Giving people what they want" is cheap and base, and the preacher who is afraid to struggle against traditional culture which holds the Word captive is unworthy of his calling. But "giving people what they *don't* want" is equally mean and low when that means putting the desire to punish above the desire to proclaim.

When the gospel is lost in a senseless struggle over cultural tastes, then the true progress of the cause of Christ in the community is often set back a dozen years. Worse, the people may become permanently confused over what the real point of the gospel is—some deciding to defend tradition forever while others commit themselves to a lifelong crusade for constant change, whatever it is. Usually everyone has past religious experiences that cause him to lean one way or the other. If encouraged by a misguided preacher—whether a dogged tradition-defender or a dedicated iconoclast—a church can be totally torn apart and almost permanently misled.

Impact, then, must result from the eternal Word encountering contemporary man. If committed to hearing and declaring the still unheard and ever-radical word of God, the preacher can never be so bound to tradition that noncommunication and boredom ensue; nor can he be so committed to overturning everything familiar that he drives people into communicative *shock* and actually prevents the progress he professes to love. When attached to the proper basis, *communion* is an essential feature of Christian communication. The deep trust it builds encourages people to open themselves to the true impact of the gospel. Understanding the functions of communion, impact, and shock can prevent needless tedium and bloodshed in the church and save the preacher from wasting his ministry in mindless wars on the cultural periphery.

Having briefly examined the interworkings of these three concepts, we must now see how the form of the sermon and the language of the sermon influence the communication of the gospel and produce either impact, boredom, or shock.

7

THE WORD BECOMES FLESH

The ultimate test for incarnational preaching comes at that moment when proclamation ceases to be theoretical and takes on flesh and blood as the sermon. When preaching dwells among us, then we know whether it really is what it gives itself out to be. We only know preaching as the sermons we have heard, not as a pure, disembodied ideal. This means that preaching cannot avoid the crucial and difficult question of the form of the sermon.

If incarnational preaching is not to remain an abstract ideal, we are faced with the necessity of finding a form that allows it to become a living reality. Whatever the shape of this kind of preaching, it is evident that it must take seriously both the historic revelation and the contemporary situation. But these two poles are never more powerful in their attraction than in the influence each of them wields over the possible shape of the sermon. A cluster of methods has gathered about each pole, and each has attracted equally prominent and serious exponents.

For example, those preachers whose confessional tradition or theological positions have primarily attracted them to the *historic given* of proclamation favor forms which suit that emphasis. Since the text of the Scripture is greatly emphasized, they tend toward expository preaching and often toward deductive stances. The homily is frequently the form of choice. They believe that the Bible is the only proper starting place for the

THE WORD BECOMES FLESH

sermon. And since the proper order is always God-man, a heavy downward movement is evident in the structure of these sermons. Frequently such "human devices" as illustrations, introductions, and topical themes are downgraded.

Karl Barth is the classic example of this emphasis. He insists that the preacher must be faithful both to the text and to life, but "it is always better to keep too close to the text" if a choice must be made.[1] Again, "the movement does not consist so much in going toward men as in coming from Christ to meet them. Preaching therefore proceeds downward."[2]

On the other hand, those preachers who are naturally attracted to the *contemporary given* of the preaching task favor person-centered, life-situation, inductive preaching forms. This emphasis frequently magnifies the use of literature, innovative forms, illustrations, contemporary applications, and involvement with current issues.

Historically, Harry Emerson Fosdick probably comes to mind first, but he has a crowd of others around him who believe that the contemporary post of the hermeneutical arch is the proper end of the bridge from which to begin. Fosdick definitely believed in the use of the Bible in his preaching (and he specifically repudiated topical preaching[3]), but he believed that the proper starting place for the sermon was the problems of people. In his famous article, "What's the Matter with Preaching?" in *Harper's Magazine*, July, 1928, he wrote: "Start with a life issue, a real problem, personal or social, perplexing the mind or disturbing the conscience; face that problem fairly, deal with it honestly, and throw such light on it from the spirit of Christ, that people will be able to think more clearly and live more nobly because of that sermon."

Both of these positions have enthusiastic, sometimes even fierce, defenders. I would not question for a moment the earnestness of these convictions (I haven't got the courage!), nor the validity of many of their insights. Nevertheless, I must insist that any attempt at resolving the tension in proclamation between the historic and the contemporary will prove unsatisfactory.

Both of these efforts are attempts to guarantee that Christian proclamation will occur because of an approach. But that is impossible. *No homiletical hedge about the gospel can insure the contact between the human and the divine.* There is no form that can guarantee proclamational correctness. The homily cannot do it; expository preaching cannot do it. The devil had his mouth full of Scripture when he tempted Jesus in the wilderness, but he never spoke the truth. Nor can life-situation preaching, or dialogical preaching, or inductive preaching guarantee proclamation. These approaches may interest, intrigue, or involve the listener—but in what? Is interesting preaching, even shared preaching, always relevant preaching? Can relevance be guaranteed by form?

Any sermon form that ignores either the historic revelation or the contemporary situation violates the incarnational nature of proclamation.

Even when one of these approaches does not ignore the Bible or the people, but only places its dominant focus upon one or the other, it still cannot be regarded as *the* answer to sermon form. Since none of these approaches—inductive or deductive, life situation or expository—*defines* preaching, none of them can *equal* preaching. Depending on the man, the text, and the congregation, any number of approaches might be preferred. But since preaching cannot be equated with any one method, no one method can dictate the form of the sermon.

The preacher has been partly intimidated by terminology, most of which is utterly meaningless to him in the first place. He hears of "expository" preaching, "textual" preaching, "topical" preaching—but what does that mean? How much text does it take to turn a "textual" sermon into an "expository" sermon? How little text to turn a "textual" sermon into a "topical" sermon? Can "expository" sermons have topics? Can "topical" sermons have texts? What is an "expository" sermon? Is it how much attention the preacher gives his text? If so, then how much attention, and what kind, does it take to qualify a sermon as "expository"? Or how little, before it is merely (perish the thought!) "topical"? Or is it *what kind* of attention he gives his text? If he parses all of the words in fifty-four verses of Scripture, is it an "expository" sermon? Must he present the verses in order? What if he finds a unifying theme or, to use an ugly word, a subject? No wonder some preachers have become altogether cynical about sermon form!

Even more intimidating than "expository preaching" is the more recent term, "biblical preaching" ("I am of Apollos; I am of Cephas; but I am of Christ!" [1 Cor. 1:12]). But what is *biblical* preaching? Is that something different from expository preaching?

But isn't that exactly the problem? Isn't "biblical preaching" redundant? In fact, is it not true that there is no "biblical preaching," there is only *preaching*? Can there be any preaching that is not biblical? That is, preaching that is ultimately independent of the historic revelation? Or for that matter, can there be any preaching that is not life-centered? Obviously there can be addresses from the pulpit which are one or the other, or neither, but is this *preaching*?

Preaching is an applied word; a term which, in the Christian setting, sustains the closest possible relationship with the content of its message, and therefore one which cannot be separated from that message without losing its meaning altogether. Nor can Christian preaching be separated from life, abstract, remote, impersonal. The nature of the Christian message itself demands that.

All of which simply means that limiting modifiers on the word *preaching*, such as "biblical" or "life-situation," may be necessary at times as correctives on the practice of Christian preaching, but *they do not really add to its meaning*. Nor should they be understood as *limiting* the sermon; as if "biblical" preaching should ignore the human setting or "life-situation" preaching should ignore the Bible.

When preaching seems to forget the Good News it has to tell, then perhaps it needs to hear of "biblical" preaching; and similarly, when preaching forgets that it must minister to the changing, complex problems of contemporary people, then perhaps it needs to hear of "life-situation" preaching. But neither alters the intrinsic nature of preaching. Likewise, "incarnational" preaching adds nothing to the nature of Christian proclamation; this expression is merely another attempt to call our attention to the true nature of preaching itself.

Each of the clusters of methods which have gathered about the historical pole and the contemporary pole have worthy insights. Those on the historical side recognize the importance of the Christian message and the necessity of working carefully with the biblical text; those on the contemporary side recognize the necessity for grappling with the flesh-and-blood problems of real people. As a result, the specific approaches to preaching suggested by each emphasis should be regarded as useful methods rather than exclusive, definitive statements on preaching.

Any of these approaches to sermon development—inductive or deductive, life-situation preaching or expository preaching, the rhetorical sermon or the homily—can be useful forms for Christian preaching, so long as their emphases do not become so one-sided that they do violence to the nature of preaching itself.

What then, if anything, can the preacher do to insure his preaching at this point? If no particular form of the sermon can guarantee Christian proclamation, is the preacher left without any guidelines at all? What principles can he follow in developing fresh forms for preaching?

Two elements affect the nature of the sermon: the substance of the message, and the shape of the message. Let us examine some principles that are basic to each.

The Message: Substance

First, we may state *two basic principles which regulate the content of the sermon:* (1) the sermon must not be separated from the historic revelation; (2) the sermon must not be separated from the contemporary situation. In fact, since the historic revelation and the contemporary situation are inherent to preaching itself, we might go so far as to say that preaching *cannot* be separated from these things and still remain preaching. Let us see what implications these principles have for the nature of the sermon.

(1) *Preaching must not be separated from the historic revelation.* If preaching becomes separated from the historic revelation of God, what is the norm for the Christian message? Are all utterances Christian? What is to determine a Christian message from a non-Christian message? Like it or not, the Christian preacher is inescapably bound to the Bible. If the spirit which speaks to us does not say that which Jesus said, it is not his Spirit (John 14:26; 15:26). We preach not ourselves, but Christ. And the Christ which we preach is defined by the historical Jesus of Nazareth.

With all of the difficulties and problems of hermeneutical effort, there is no escaping that struggle. It is just as wrong for the preacher to absolutely abandon any attempt at interpreting the meaning of the historical Christ for us as it is for him to believe that a particular interpretative system can objectively capture his Spirit. Therefore Christian preaching has been, and ought to continue to be, connected with original language studies and exegesis. Bonhoeffer and Bultmann are as emphatic at that point as is Barth.

Again, this does not mean that taking a text insures Christian proclamation. Many a sermon "takes a text, departs therefrom, and returns not thereunto." That is one reason so many people have only the vaguest notion what Christianity is all about, like the old woman who always cried whenever she heard the word *Mesopotamia.* A sermon may be full of texts but empty of the gospel. Every cult and heresy from the first century on has been long on proof-texts and short on authentic interpretation. Meaningful preaching must speak the vital, lively message of the Bible rather than using its texts as a pack of spiritual Tarot cards for Christian fortune-telling.

Spurgeon said it well: "I know a minister whose shoe latchet I am unworthy to unloose, whose preaching is often little better than sacred miniature painting—I might almost say holy trifling. He is great upon the ten toes of the beast, the four faces of the cherubim, the mystical meaning of badgers' skins, and the typical bearings of the staves of the ark, and the windows of Solomon's temple: but the sins of business men, the temptations of the times, and the needs of the age, he scarcely ever touches upon. Such preaching reminds me of a lion engaged in mouse-hunting. . . ."[4]

"Holy trifling" does nothing to impress the importance of the Bible upon the congregation; in fact, this insignificant handling of the Scripture actually diminishes the significance of the word of God for the real problems of real people.

Conversely, it is possible for preaching to occur without the reading of a text. Bonhoeffer insisted that Luther often preached without a text, yet nevertheless biblically. If the message that is delivered is informed by the authentic message of the Bible or the true spirit of Christ himself—not any Christ, but *Jesus* Christ—then preaching has occurred. But even then, the revealed Word has resulted in the spoken word, if indirectly. We continue to affirm the actions of God.

For example, when Fosdick "took his text from Broadway," why did he choose to examine one particular line from a play over the others he had heard? It was because the note of reality it struck echoed the note of biblical revelation. But if brought into question, every message must be able to establish itself as gospel. And therefore, whether immediately or ultimately, preaching can never be separated from the historic revelation.

(2) *Preaching must not be separated from the contemporary situation.* Because there is a human factor in the preaching equation, the sermon must confront the personal and corporate problems which people face. The sermon must involve itself with analysis of the human situation, illustration of the principles of the gospel in terms of contemporary life, and application of the word of God to the specific situations. Therefore psychology and sociology can serve as useful tools in the exegesis of the human situation just as critical methodology serves as a useful tool in the exegesis of the text. Our understanding of the human condition facilitates analysis of the living situation and the application of the gospel to life.

We may agree with Ott when he says that this interpretation must be done without the sermon "deteriorating into a simple amplification of human self-judgments on the basis of moral, sociological, psycho-analytic criteria and such like"; yet these sciences may help us to do that which Ott suggests: "The picture must be drawn concretely, with reference to the daily life of men just as it is. . . . It must be brought home to him in concrete illustration, that he may accept it."[5]

Our sermons cannot reflect profound knowledge of the first century and abysmal ignorance of the twentieth century. No one can be true to the biblical text and ignore the congregation. The biblical word is never a word in abstraction. It is always a specific word to a specific situation. Jesus used concrete language from his contemporary situation to incarnate his ultimate revelation. However it is done, "applying to life" is essential to proclamation.

This becomes increasingly difficult for the preacher as life becomes more complex and as provincialism becomes less acceptable. Fifty years ago H. V. Kaltenborn, managing editor of the Brooklyn *Eagle*, had a sign on his desk that said that a dogfight in Brooklyn was more important than a revolution in China. That was never true, but the ridiculousness of the statement becomes more evident every day.

But how can the pastor be specific in his preaching? How can the church speak the commandments, as Bonhoeffer has urged? Can the preacher "know" about the school board, the UN, the police force, the local housing and zoning ordinances, the water and sewage system, the Congress and the Supreme Court? Maybe; a little; and no. Obviously he cannot be an authority on all subjects. What then?

The church must be specific, but what does that mean— doctrinaire pronouncements on everything, whether ignorant or not? Or should the sermon be forced into vagueness, withdrawal, and eventual silence?

If preaching is to be truly incarnational, then the pastor must be involved with human life; and to the degree that he is, his sermon will be also. His preaching must be specific enough to incarnate the Word in the contemporary. But it must also understand that it cannot play answer-man to the world. The principles of the gospel must not be left in abstraction, but neither can the pastor apply texts like Band-Aids to every specific dilemma of every member of the congregation.

Concretely illustrating and specifically applying the gospel to life, however, translates the gospel from the idiom of the first century to the idiom of the twentieth century. By so doing, application assists in the interpretation of the Word. Faith is then made possible, since "faith cometh by hearing, and hearing by the word of God" (Rom. 10:17).

And through faith-action on the part of the church—the believing people of God—specific application of the gospel by the congregation can occur in countless situations about which the pastor could not even know, much less comprehend. *This is the true concretion of the message.*

Must specific problems be discussed in detail in every sermon in order for preaching not to be separated from the contemporary situation? No, I think we must take some recognition of the emphatic insistence of both Barth and Bonhoeffer that the word of God provides a concrete application in itself. Just as a text must not always be quoted directly in order for a sermon to be Christian proclamation, so a sermon may be intimately connected with human life without analyzing particulars of the contemporary setting.

But I think we need to realize that both of these statements merely set the outer limits for Christian proclamation; they are not normative for it. There is no need for seeing how near the edge we can drive the sermon without falling off. Preaching without reference to Scripture is a dubious practice, and so is preaching without reference to the human situation. The most enthusiastic advocates of either textual explanation or analysis of the human situation rarely resorted to these extremes. For example, Barth's sermons consistently included references to the contemporary situation, and illustrations as well, and Fosdick's sermons averaged about a dozen references to the Bible.[6]

The determinative question for Christian preaching is not

how much biblical reference is made, nor *how much* contemporary reference, but whether the circuit is closed between the Word of God and the situation of man. Preaching must commit itself to both, realizing that *when the living Word touches the living situation, the preaching event occurs.* Any approach to the sermon which does not separate itself from one or the other permits the possibility of preaching.

The Message: Shape

These two principles speak to the content of the sermon. But content is not the only influence on the nature of the sermon. The arrangement of these materials, the order—or lack of it—in which the presentation is made, determines the shape of the sermon. Four basic principles may help the preacher to arrive at a form that facilitates preaching: Communication requires form; the form employed must be capable of conveying a message; the message demands a dynamic rather than a static form; the dynamic form of the sermon requires the oral medium.

(1) *Communication requires form.* Without organization, communication is impossible. This is true of the message as a whole, or of a sentence, or even of a single word. For example, the letters *T-R-E-E*, in that order, communicate an image, but *E-E-T-R* communicates nothing. And that which is true of a single word is also true of the arrangement of words within a sentence, or of thoughts within a sermon.

Because of the difficulty of arriving at satisfactory organization, the preacher is tempted toward formlessness. The freedom that is within the gospel and within himself struggles against form. But whether the form chosen is innovative or traditional, the message which is within the preacher must assume some form of expression or it cannot be communicated at all.

Form is essential to freedom. A certain humility is required of the artist who must limit himself to a particular medium, to the particularization of his vision in a given form on canvas or clay or stone. But as limited as that expression may be, without it he cannot communicate at all. There is no music without sound, no poetry without words, no art without shape. These forms set the vision free by giving expression to it. Without the sculpture, Michelangelo's *David* would be more trapped in his mind than it was in the stone.

(2) *The form employed must be capable of conveying a message.* Preaching is declaring the Good News. Not all forms of communication are equally adapted to this end. In his examination of those forms best suited to the expression of the Christian message, Paul Tillich prefers Expressionism, rather than Impressionism or Romanticism, since "that which is expressed is not the subjectivity of the artist in the sense of the subjective element which is predominant in Impressionism and Romanticism."[7] The gospel confronts us with reality, and the form of the sermon must be suited to the communication of that reality; Romanticism idealizes it too much, and Impressionism makes it too arbitrarily subjective.

On the other hand, Realism also fails as a form because it merely repeats without interpreting. Expressing the reality of the gospel does not imply a mere parroting of words—which may explain why *keryx*, or herald, is almost never used as the word for "preacher" in the New Testament; the ancient herald was widely regarded as nothing more than a paid parrot. The preacher, however, must be involved with the message he bears and the people to whom he bears it. Not merely repetition, but interpretation is required to communicate the reality of the Christian message.

Nonetheless, it is not *any* message, but *that* message which we have to communicate. In defending certain experimental sermons against the charge that "they go too far and in some instances actually alter the original message of Christianity," John Killinger correctly reminds us that we must not commit the fallacy of focusing too closely on the dogmatic formulations of the Christian gospel and miss the total meaning and spirit of that message. But if it is true that "man is a free spirit and must not be indentured to any system," it is only the message of the gospel which liberates him. "If you continue in my word, then are you my disciples indeed; and you shall know the truth, and the truth shall make you free" (John 8:31–32). Indeed, it is "God, in Christ," and him alone, who has "called us out from all totalitarian superstructures;" therefore we must question whether "our first obligation now is to our own centers of freedom."[8]

What is freedom? Rudolf Bultmann insists that "genuine freedom is not subjective arbitrariness. It is freedom in obedience. . . . Genuine freedom is freedom from the motivation of the moment; it is freedom which withstands the clamor and pressure of momentary motivations." Likewise, he reminds us that this idea of freedom, constituted by law, was well known to both ancient Greek philosophy and Christianity, but that "in modern times, however, this conception vanished and was replaced by the illusory idea of freedom as subjective arbitrariness which does not acknowledge a norm, a law from beyond. There insues a realitivism which does not acknowledge absolute ethical demands and absolute truth. The end of this development is nihilism."[9]

This leads us to question also whether language in preaching can become so open-ended and playful that it is "committed to the game, not to the end in view. . . . It does not manifest high control needs, but abandons itself to the activity and to whatever outcome eventuates."[10] But is "whatever outcome eventuates" invariably the gospel? And are we in fact manifesting "high control needs" if we use language "to reach certain goals which we already had in mind when we began"?[11] If so, are there *any* sermon forms that communicate which have no end in view and therefore are nonpurposive? *Especially* experimental sermon forms, which usually demand the mastery of art forms such as poetry or drama, that in fact require more careful planning and structured use of language than the traditional forms.

I think it is true that we must allow language "to lead us along paths where knowledge is uncertain, revealing new worlds to us in the process."[12] This is indeed highly important. I will attempt to suggest an approach to preparation which facilitates this process. But creativity and absolute spontaneity are evidently not synonymous.

In any event, the form chosen for the sermon—whether experimental or traditional—should not become identified with purposeless speech or subjective arbitrariness, but it must be capable of conveying the Christian message.

(3) *The message demands a dynamic rather than a static form.* To insist upon meaningful form for the sermon is not to insist upon a rigid shape for the message. Some forms are dynamic and fluid; others are static and lifeless.

A brick and a flame both have form, but there is reason why a brick is not as interesting to watch as a flame. The brick is static, it has no movement, but the flame is lively, changing, intriguing. That is the reason we watch the flames in the fireplace on long winter evenings rather than the bricks around it. Nevertheless, fire has form; combustion is as specific a reality as stone.

Preaching must be constantly in search for dynamic forms to express the dynamic reality of the gospel. All traditional methods of preaching were once new and innovative, and communication demands a spirit of inventiveness: "Real communication is not static; it can seldom be accomplished for very long without experimentation and innovation."[13]

For many preachers, unfortunately, seminary training in preaching merely furnished them with a set of homiletical cookie cutters which they routinely mash down upon the dough of the text, and presto! out pops a little star, or a tree, or a gingerbread man (a five-pointed sermon? an organic sermon? a life-situation sermon?). No matter that the text doesn't want to go into these forms; the poor thing is mashed and tortured until it is made to say things it never intended to say.

There is nothing wrong with any of these forms in themselves, the crime is the dully mechanical and arbitrary way in which they are imposed upon the text. As much as possible, the shape of the reality encountered in the gospel should determine the shape of the sermon. At times traditional forms may best express that reality, but, depending upon the preacher, the text, and the congregation, innovative approaches might well be demanded.

The redeeming principle, however, is neither innovation nor traditionalism, but that we *shape the sermon in a living form that brings to expression the living reality of the gospel.*

(4) *The dynamic form of the sermon requires the oral medium.* Nothing so facilitates the dynamic nature of preaching as the oral medium. Even experimental forms, if written into fixed sentence formulation, can become static. And nothing so lulls a congregation into passivity as the "whoosh" of the opening of a canned, hermetically sealed sermon—whether traditional or not. Unless the oral medium is taken seriously, the most innovative sermon forms with the most profound sermon content will be static. And as such, they violate the essential nature of preaching itself as personal encounter.

To a greater or lesser degree, preaching theories have generally recognized the historic revelation and the contemporary situation as essential to the sermon. But the recognition of preaching as word-event, and particularly as an *acoustic* event, has been much slower in coming. Preaching is not merely a *verbal* event, it is an *oral* event. Verbal communication may be either written or oral; but as we have seen, in the history of Israel and in the preaching of the early church there is no mistaking the preferred method of communication.

Nor was that incidental. Oral communication permits dynamic personal encounter, and that is not at all incidental to preaching. And it does so to a degree far above written communication because of its immediacy. Of course all sermons are spoken, but as we shall see, not all sermons are really constructed to fit the oral medium.

Since the sermon is spoken, it must be shaped to suit the oral medium. That is as essential to the communication of the gospel as the correct interpretation of the biblical text or the contemporary situation. First preaching learned that it must take the text seriously; then it learned that it must take the people seriously; now it must learn that it must take the medium seriously.

8

OUT OF THE GUTENBERG GALAXY

Following the nineteenth century and the advent of popular literacy, the sermon was steadily transformed from its original oral medium into a literary, written medium. This change was partly due to the impact of printing as a medium for communication, and partly due to the sensational success of the "comets in the Gutenberg galaxy"—to play with McLuhan's term—the literary preachers to that literary age.

The influence of these men upon the form of the modern sermon is incalculable. The sermons of Robertson, Spurgeon, and others were printed and distributed to millions. Homileticians subsequently used those written sermons as models of excellence for their preaching classes. And although this approach unquestionably produced many good results, it also had one unfortunate effect upon the sermon. Students were encouraged, directly or indirectly, to *write* sermons like the ones they were reading.

As a result, the sermon was increasingly prepared for the eye rather than the ear. Devices suited for reading—paragraphing, formal syntax, tightly fitted logical arguments, complex outlines, literary language—were superimposed upon the sermon. Of course the sermon continued to be delivered orally, but increasingly from a manuscript really prepared for reading.

Like a satellite trapped within the gravitational pull of a planet, preaching has been locked into the Gutenberg galaxy.

The sermon must break out of this orbit if it is to be able to communicate within its own medium.

The methods of the nineteenth-century preachers were largely effective for their age, but they have become increasingly less so as culture has shifted its interest. This is the reason many preachers sound sadly Victorian, or like chaplains to a literary society. What has happened to the sermon is what McLuhan also describes—*the lively communication medium for one generation has become the art form for the next generation.*

McLuhan's theories, like his writings, are often more suggestive than logical, but they may help us to explain the situation in which preaching finds itself. For example, McLuhan says that as man develops new media for communication his relationship to the old medium changes. The new environment created by the new media causes the old medium to become an art form.

Many questions could be raised about McLuhan's division of civilization into three ages, the Preliterate or Tribal, the Gutenberg or Individual, and the Electric or Retribalized, and the order in which each of the senses became dominant—first the ear, hearing; then the eye, seeing; now the central nervous system, total sensory experience. Nevertheless, according to this sytem, speaking was the dominant medium of communication in the aural, or Preliterate age; printing was the dominant medium during the visual, or the Gutenberg age; and the telegraph, telephone, and television have become the dominant media during the Electronic age.

Obviously this explanation tends to be simplistic; the use of our senses is not so neatly layered, nor is the function of the media. But like most of McLuhan's themes these suggestions are stimulating and provocative, and it is interesting to pursue their implications for the development of communication in the church.

Let us accept for a moment these two suppositions—that various senses become dominant in various ages and produce a dominant medium of communication, and that the dominant communication medium of one age becomes the art form of the next age. What does this theory suggest for preaching?

Speaking was the dominant communication medium in the Hebrew-Christian tradition, in the biblical centuries. The art form for that age was the temple ritual, the Passover celebration, and other liturgical acts which celebrated the past events of that tradition. As printing became the new dominant medium for communication in succeeding ages, speaking was changed from a medium of communication to an art form—oratory. At first the church was intimidated by printing. But soon that changed, and preachers began to capitalize upon it with the result that the sermon was increasingly prepared with the eye in mind rather than the ear; that is, with the thought of possible publication.

At first that was a realistic option, both in England and in the early American colonies. A staple diet of the colonial press was pamphlet sermons, and more than 40 percent of the entries in Evan's *American Bibliography* were sermons.[1] But as the electronic media came into being, consumption of printed sermons dropped radically. Soon the only consumers of sermons were those who sat and listened to the spoken sermon. *Then the manuscripted sermon, prepared according to the rules of writing to suit the printing medium, became the art form of preaching.*

Even today, when the possibilities for publication of any one Sunday's sermon are infinitely small, preachers continue to prepare their messages for one medium and deliver them in another. It is not incidental that the manuscript is widely regarded as the final product of the preacher's *art*. If today's preaching is not regarded as a lively form of communication, part of the blame at least must be attached to the manuscripted sermon—the art form of homiletics.

This would not be true if the principles for written and oral communication were alike. But they are not. For example, everyone has noticed that even the finest oral communications generally look horrible when transcribed. John Broadus preached an excellent series of sermons at Calvary Church in

New York which he was urged to publish, but when he saw the stenographer's transcription of them he was so horrified that he called off the project. Many of us have had similar experiences. But does this mean that the sermon was done poorly in the first place? Not at all. It simply means that what suits the ear does not suit the eye.

What about the corollary of that law? Has it ever occurred to us that if spoken speeches look bad when transcribed, the opposite might also be true—*that written speeches sound bad when heard*? There are really no exceptions to this law although we've all heard sermons from manuscripts which seem to be. But in those cases, the manuscript has been forced to make radical concessions to the spoken medium.

What are the major differences between oral and written style? Even a partial listing should help us to understand the problem.[2]

In the first place, the primary difference is that one style is intended for the eye and the other for the ear. A reader has time to ponder, reread, and even look up words if necessary; a hearer must understand the message as it comes or not at all. A reader may proceed at his own pace; a listener goes at the pace of the speaker. If writing does not proceed in linear style, a reader gets bored; but if a speaker avoids repetition, his listener gets lost if concentration is broken even for a moment.

Furthermore, written style is arranged according to the needs of the eye. It uses paragraphing and formal syntax. Paragraphs are useful to the eye, but they have no meaning to the ear. Written style needs formal syntax to avoid confusion. Until the age of printing, punctuation was used for nothing more than an opportunity for a speaker to take a breath. But printing necessitated the use of commas and periods to set off clauses for the eye, and McLuhan says that the curse of English grammar is a direct consequence of the printing press.[3]

Even more decisive for preaching, McLuhan points out that when words are printed they become visual, static elements and lose much of the dynamism which characterizes the auditory world. They lose much of the personal element in the

emotional overtones and emphases of the spoken word.[4] In oral
communication the speaker and the listener are in interreaction
within the situation, but writing prevents such a response.[5]

It is also interesting to note that McLuhan suggests that Jesus
did not commit his teachings to writing because "the kind of
interplay of life that is in teaching is not possible by means of
writing."[6] And he quotes Thomas Aquinas as saying, "Therefore it is fitting that Christ, as the most excellent teacher,
should adapt that manner of teaching whereby his doctrine
would be imprinted on the hearts of his hearers."[7]

But do listeners know the difference between "oral" and
"nonoral" sermons? They do. An audience can successfully
label a speech as being "oral" or "nonoral" in style even
though they only hear the nonoral version of the speech, or the
oral, and when they are not given a definition of what consti-
tutes an oral style.[8] Furthermore, listeners find oral speeches to
be more understandable, more interesting, more informative,
and superior in style.

To overcome these difficulties, teachers of preaching have
long advocated "writing like you speak." But that is a hybrid
art that nobody teaches. Learning to speak and learning to write
are difficult enough in themselves without learning to hybri-
dize the two. And why do it anyway? Why not prepare for the
oral medium in the first place?

The preacher should realize that his problems don't stop
once he has written his manuscript; in fact, they have just
begun. Then he *really* has a problem. What does he *do* with it?

He is faced with three alternatives—all bad: (1) He can read
it. Nobody recommends that, for obvious reasons. (2) He can
memorize it. Nobody recommends that either. (3) Or he can get
familiar with it as much as possible in the study and then try to
do without it as much as possible in the pulpit. This third
alternative is the method generally recommended. But it still
leaves the preacher with plenty of trouble.

When a preacher is trying to follow a manuscript mentally,
without taking it with him, he presents a curious sight. When
he is successful in recalling his material, he sounds polished

and looks poised—sometimes too polished and too poised, like a boy delivering a piece learned for school. On the other hand, when he is unsuccessful, his word choice and syntax are radically different. He may also have a vacant look on his face as he frantically rummages around in his mental attic trying to remember all those beautiful phrases he wrote and rewrote in his study.

Meanwhile, of course, his mouth has to go on working. But he isn't too happy about it, and so he may look slightly irritated, which in turn may cause his audience to wonder what they have done to offend him. Nevertheless, there is nothing to do but plunge on, and so he proceeds into the next section of his material. But then he may abruptly remember those well-written phrases he needed five minutes earlier. Unless he is an unusual man, he will give in to the temptation to go ahead and say them anyway, in place or not, causing his audience to wonder how in the world he got back on *that* subject. The whole procedure gives preaching a curious, disjointed effect.

As for the man who takes his manuscript with him and tries not to look at it, he usually looks like a man trying not to look at a manuscript. He may struggle manfully to look his audience in the eye, but it is apparent that his heart is not in it, and he keeps sneaking furtive glances at the pages beneath his fingers. If he is bold enough to go ahead and look anyway, he often gives the effect of a Kiwi bird going to water. Now his head is up, now his head is down. Meanwhile, his audience sits respectfully listening, as though hearing a sermon required great politeness—which in this case, it does. Active mental dialogue and personal encounter give way to polite listening.

I know that some men can master the use of a manuscript so that their delivery is smooth and natural. Many of the finest preachers in Christian history preached exclusively from manuscripts. I know that. But that doesn't eliminate the problems I have described. They are still there, and the manuscript preachers who excel do so in spite of their manuscripts, not because of them.

For years preachers have been intimidated by the "ideal" of

these great preachers and their polished manuscripts. They have been asked, "Isn't preaching worth the effort? Can we afford to go into the pulpit half-prepared?" Karl Barth has even warned darkly that we will be held accountable for every idle word in the day of judgment and used this Scripture as a proof-text for the absolute necessity of a manuscript.[9] (We will not take this as a typical example of the great exegete.) Naturally he equates anything else with a lack of preparation.

But are these really the alternatives? Is it preparation versus unpreparation, the careful manuscript versus the offhanded talk? Is there no other approach which prepares a man as carefully and as thoroughly as the manuscript, or more so, and which connects him more directly with the true oral medium for the sermon?

The Oral Manuscript

Let me suggest a method that I believe to be superior to the writing of a manuscript. I know that all men are not alike, and there is no method which is best for everyone. In spite of what ought to be true, some men might be helpless without a manuscript. But I don't believe that it is the best method for most men. Anyone who uses a manuscript should realize that he is not merely using a crutch, he is putting a brace on a healthy leg.

I am convinced that much of the stiffness and impersonality of our preaching, the boredom and lack of interest of our hearers, the feeling of nonparticipation and disinvolvement of our congregations, is due to the manuscript method of preaching. (It would be ridiculous to attribute these problems to manuscript preparation alone; but to my knowledge, it has scarcely been pointed out as any part of the problem at all, and I believe it is much more to blame methodologically for our troubles than the often ridiculed, "three-point," traditional organization.)

I repeat: In those cases where the method has been mastered and a man is able to communicate intimately and directly with his congregation, he does so in spite of his manuscript and in the face of overwhelming odds against him.

On the other hand, I am equally well aware of the disastrous effects of nonpreparation. There is nothing more deadly to preaching than the man who can say nothing for thirty minutes, and knows it. If forced to choose between listening to this man with the rotary jaw, to use Spurgeon's term, or to the poor reading of a well-prepared manuscript, I'd choose the manuscript every time. If the preacher had to choose between doing without careful sermon preparation and doing without direct contact with his audience, I suppose he should do without direct contact with his audience. But that's like deciding which of your children to shoot. You don't have to make that choice.

In looking for a better procedure, where do we begin? (At this point, perhaps I had better warn you that we are only going to look at the overall process for the sake of clarity; the details of mechanics will come later.)

Initial Study. The oral preparation method begins exactly like the manuscript method. First, the preacher should make a careful study of his text—which involves both exegetical and meditative study—and establish a tentative plan for the sermon in rough notes. This plan includes no more at this time than the unifying concern, or direction, or theme of the sermon, and a tentative arrangement of the basic divisions or steps in the development of this theme.

To this point, the preparation of the sermon is a matter of thought, but beyond this early stage it should be a matter of speech. The tentative direction of the sermon which thought has suggested should be made definite through speaking. We begin with the rough oral draft.

The Rough Oral Draft. Put each of the tentative divisions of the theme on a separate sheet of paper. Then preach aloud on each of them as long as ideas suggest themselves, using free association. Make no effort to hinder the free flow of ideas or to arrange them in order at this time. But keep a pen in hand and pause in speaking only long enough to note briefly the key directional phrases or sentences that emerge.

Each of these sentences should introduce a *thought-block*

which has really struck the heart of the concern of the text or of the people. These phrases correspond with the topic sentence of the paragraphs in a manuscript. But in this case they do not introduce a paragraph—no one speaks in paragraphs—but a thought-block, "something I want to talk about," which may represent one or more minutes of oral development.

This stage corresponds exactly with the writing of the rough draft of the manuscript—*except that it is being done in the medium which will eventually be used.* The composition is oral, not written, and the difference can be plainly heard in the final product. Verbal fluency will jump dramatically using this method. And rather than practicing on your audience, you are practicing on yourself.

Furthermore, a man can speak at least five to ten times faster than he can write. A written rough draft of the number of words used in the oral process would take just that much longer; a two-hour oral session would require at least a ten-hour written session. This means valuable time saved, and a more efficient use of sermon preparation time with this approach.

It is important to remember that the initial arrangement of divisions, or even your understanding of the basic sermon theme itself, will very likely be altered as the speaking process unfolds. These ideas are highly tentative; they serve only as a starting point for the sermon. You will often discover that your initial impression has been clarified and refined in the speaking process. Don't hesitate to alter the pieces to say what you want to say. Many a preacher has been trapped by a "logical" outline that would not let him speak the gospel as he understood it.

In this rough draft stage, you will not know what to say first within each division—should I start with the biblical situation or with the contemporary situation?—or whether some pictorial, illustrative material should be used before either is introduced. But talking it out allows you to *hear it, try it,* and then decide.

Sometimes you may preach aloud for fifteen minutes or more on each division before you say anything worth saying. (At least you will find that out in the study rather than in the pulpit! How often a preacher practices on his congregation—and learns five minutes before the end what he should have said in the first place!) It will be a common experience to realize suddenly, "That's what I've been trying to say!" Not only the organization, but the very meaning of the message is being discovered in the speaking process.

Once the basic content of the sermon is set, decide how to begin—the introduction—and how to stop—the conclusion. Then when you have finished this process of preparation, the rough draft of the oral manuscript is completed.

The Final Oral Manuscript. At this point, what do you have? A few lines to begin; perhaps a few to conclude. A *few main divisions,* if these are necessary to move the sermon through the meaning of the message. Under these key divisions, *several directional sentences* that introduce thought-blocks; some which deal with the biblical situation, some which deal with the contemporary situation, and some which may also indicate the use of pictorial, illustrative material, or the need for it.

Then what? Examine your notes. Rearrange the directional sentences, and perhaps even the main divisions themselves, into the order which seemed called for by the speaking process.

For example, on the first run you may have discovered that the second division should have been first; or that it really said the same thing as the first and therefore is not needed at all. Or within the first division, you may have begun with a narrative based on the text and led into a contemporary narrative; but in doing so, it quickly became apparent that this order was awkward and should be reversed. Or, as the rough oral draft unfolded, you may have jotted down a dozen sentences under the first division which seemed to introduce promising areas of thought, only three or four of which actually proved to be worth keeping. In other words, having heard your sermon, you are now able to revise it.

If you are reasonably satisfied that this revised arrangement permits the gospel to be heard, then preach aloud once more. *This is the final draft of the oral manuscript.* Obviously you will continue to revise if necessary, but this time you are attempting to preach in as near final form as possible. Sharpen the focus and the language of the message. Try to preach without reference to the material before you, but if necessary, refer to it. If your development is simple and accurate, it will not be hard to recall; if you cannot work through it easily, quite likely there is some problem with the movement of the sermon.

The Sermon Brief

You will discover that this oral process has produced an instrument for you to retain and refer to—not a sermon outline, not a sermon manuscript, but a *sermon brief*. What does the final product look like?

If there are no divisions in the sermon as in more contemporary sermon forms, the brief will simply be a page or a page and a half, likely not more, of key directional sentences, each of which introduces a thought-block of oral discussion. But if the sermon has divisions ("points"), as in traditional sermon forms, the form of the sermon brief will be slightly different.

First, there will be a *grouping* of three to five sentences which indicate the beginning of the sermon. Then the basic divisions follow, each stated as a directional sentence—something that can be *said*, rather than a "point," which generally cannot be spoken as written. Underline these sentences for clarity.

Under each of these statements, indented somewhat, follow the other directional sentences that discuss the biblical situation and the contemporary situation. (Not more than six to ten sentences at most. Remember that each of these sentences is merely a springboard to launch you into a body of thought you want to discuss.) Finally, if a conclusion is called for, it will consist of a few sentences in a block grouping, just like the introduction.

A diagram may help to illustrate this form.

Use spacing, underlining, and indenting to make the sermon brief as simple and uncluttered as possible. A good sermon

SERMON BRIEF

3–5
sentences   Introduction: _____.

Basic Directional Sentence (Division)

6–10
sentences   Key sentences,
                                       each introducing
                                       its own thought-
                                       block of discussion.
                                       (Exploring the
                                       biblical material
                                       and the contemporary
                                       situation; presenting
                                       pictorial, illustra-
                                       tive material, etc.)

Basic Directional Sentence (Division)
            (etc.)

3–5
sentences   Conclusion:

brief should be easy to visualize during preaching. The exact form of this instrument is not as critical as the form of a manuscript because it serves simply as a reminder of the oral preparation which is really the form of the sermon. But a clean, simply arranged, easily visualized brief will help the unity and movement of the message.

Any Advantages?

The sermon brief, then, is more than an outline and less than a manuscript, but in my opinion, it is superior to either. It has many advantages.

1. For one thing, the sermon has produced the instrument rather than the instrument producing the sermon, as in the case with the manuscript.

2. Furthermore, it is truer to the nature of conversation because it is less rigid, less fixed, more fluid and therefore more adaptable to the living encounter of the sermon event.

3. The sermon brief does not tie the preacher to the wording of a manuscript. It allows that freedom of creation and spontaneity of response which is essential if preaching is to be an event in the worship service. Something *happens* between preacher and congregation; everything has not already happened in the study. The manuscript gives the impression of a report on a event rather than being an event itself.

4. On the other hand, because it provides more specific direction for the sermon than a bare outline, the sermon brief does not give the impression of unpreparedness, vagueness, or aimless wandering. The preacher is not as surprised as the audience to hear what pops out of his mouth, as he often is in the purely extemporaneous method, nor does he chase rabbits through brambles for thirty minutes.

5. Finally, and most decisive, the oral process of preparation results in an oral product for the oral medium of preaching. Neither of the other methods does.

The naturalness, directness, and freedom which the preacher will enjoy in the pulpit as a result of this method will delight both himself and his congregation. I am convinced that this is more important to allow preaching to be itself—a living encounter of the living Word with the living situation—than either polished phrases or innovative forms.

Any Objections?

At least two objections are often raised against this approach. Some preachers are convinced that they will lose all freshness and enthusiasm if they speak their sermons beforehand. I have never forgotten that comment from a student who had struggled painfully to say something, *anything,* in his first sermon to his small congregation. After seven agonizing minutes, he sat down. (But no one objected—it *seemed* like an hour!) When he asked how anyone learned to talk conversationally with an audience, I suggested oral preparation. "What!" he said. "You actually say your sermon before you preach?" I assured him I did. "Why! If I did that, I'd lose all my fire!"

On the contrary, the assurance that oral preparation gives the preacher allows him to enter deeply into meaningful, exciting dialogue with his hearers. It sets him free to concentrate on the real meaning of the Word for the real people who sit before him. For the first time, perhaps, he will actually *see* people and talk *with* people, rather than looking *at* his ideas and talking *about* a subject.

Another objection might be raised. Some preachers may feel that they cannot "remember what to say" with no more than a handful of directional sentences produced by speaking. Wouldn't it help at least to tape the oral draft and play it back to remember it?

Surprisingly, perhaps, the preacher will soon discover that just the opposite is true. The problem is forgetting what you said initially, in the rough oral draft. Speaking makes an amazing impression on the memory. If you recorded the first oral draft, you would lock yourself into that pattern and revision would be extremely difficult.

But if the preacher will simply note the key directional sentences which emerge in speaking, rearrange these into the order which seems most natural and repreach the sermon in that form, he will know what he wants to say and how to say it. Only the basic pattern for the development of the sermon is to be set; during delivery variations will occur naturally in the exact wording within the thought-blocks. *But these variations are essential* for naturalness and freshness of expression.

I would suggest allowing a day or so between the rough oral draft and the final oral manuscript. Give the sermon time to grow a bit in your experience. Usually if the first draft is finished early in the week, by Wednesday at least, then Friday is a good time to talk through the material again. And even on Sunday morning before the service, the preacher would do well to mentally "preach aloud" his sermon. Creation, revision, and rearrangement really never stop—not even in the pulpit.

After this kind of oral preparation, many preachers do not need to take the sermon brief into the pulpit with them. But if the preacher feels ill at ease without it, particularly in his first few experiences with this approach, the brief will not interfere badly with his presentation. Naturally he will be freer without it, and in time he can easily learn to do without it. To prepare himself to do so, he should ask himself the following questions prior to his final oral preparation:

(1) What is the main concern of this sermon? (its purpose; theme; subject)

(2) What do I want to say about that? (order; movement; main divisions; "points")

(3) How do I begin? (opening movement)

(4) How do I proceed within the first division? the second? etc. (mental review of the order of key directional sentences)

(5) How do I conclude? (final thought-block)

When the preacher can move through each of these in his mind, he is ready to speak his sermon without notes. He will never recall every directional sentence, but that doesn't matter. What little he loses in polished phrases or content—and it will be very little, if he has prepared orally—he will gain in intimate, direct communication with his congregation.

I am aware that a great many traditional homiletical questions so far remain unanswered, and it is now time to hear what they are asking.

9

FROM THE STUDY TO THE PULPIT

At this point a number of practical questions clamor for attention. What about the traditional parts of the sermon—introduction, conclusion, titles, outlines, points, and subpoints? How do I do these things—or should I?

Even more basic, how do I find something to preach on? Where can I get ideas and material for the sermon? How do I get from a text to a sermon? And how can I deal with contemporary issues that have no direct biblical precedent?

Finally, and perhaps most critically, how do I *do* it? How can I find time in the week to prepare? And how do I plan ahead for a preaching program?

No one could feel himself homiletically messianic enough to answer all these questions. But in many pastor's conferences on preaching, these are the issues that always come up. Frankly, I don't believe them to be as desperately critical as we make them out to be. A solid approach to the Bible and to life, careful work habits, and a willingness to grow and learn will take care of most of them. In fact, no one can really answer any of these specifics for anyone else. But I am glad to express my own approach to them for whatever it is worth. It may be of some help in some areas to someone. It also may not be.

Books have been written on each of these questions. I will only touch briefly on a few of these issues to put them in perspective within this approach, and to illustrate the possibility of cohesion between a theory of proclamation and the most practical matters of sermon preparation.

I am aware that I will leave open far more packages than I will tie up with neat bows. Good. And if these methods won't work for you, so much the better. Use them if you can; step on them going on somewhere better if you can't.

It's Monday: Or, Not Again!

Getting started has to be one of the preacher's biggest headaches. Sunday has just ended—for better or worse—and he feels he deserves a vacation. But whether he takes a day off or not, Monday will still be Monday, and only the preacher knows what "a month of Sundays" means: Everytime he looks around, here comes Sunday—and another sermon. (If not two!) Then what?

Here are some rapid responses to typical questions.

How do I find something to preach about?

Year in and year out, this has got to be the question that plagues the preacher the most. What do I do when the barrel is empty?

As always, prevention is better than cure. Regular, careful listening to the Word and the people—to the historic revelation and the contemporary situation—will provide more than adequate sermon ideas and content. Learn to exegete both the Bible and the congregation. Inspiration for sermon ideas may come from either direction. This is the fundamental, long-term answer to this perennial question.

But what if a preacher feels he has *already* been aware of both of these resources and still feels "dry" of sermonic inspiration? A few practical suggestions may help a man to diagnose his own methodological needs in each area.

1. BIBLICAL SOURCES

Actually, the Bible is not a bad place to look for sermons. (But don't let that out, or everybody will get in on it.)

Study the Bible in many translations. Most of us have heard the King James so long that we don't see a third of the freshness of the biblical text. New translations show us things we've overlooked before. And read widely in the Bible. Most of us never preach from vast areas of biblical literature.

Underline the provocative expressions that stop your eye. These arresting phrases unlock doors of sermonic thought. Be sure to preach the *meaning* of those phrases in context, however, not clever essays on catchy phrases. Move from meaning to meaning, not from phrase to phrase.

Do the same with the text in original languages. Cutting corners here wastes time later. Barth said he could always tell if a preacher had studied the original texts. But be sure to truly *translate,* not transliterate, the biblical message—the *piel* and the *aorist* yield precious little preaching by themselves.

Listen long enough until you hear. Most sermons are empty because the preacher has not listened long enough before he started talking. There is nothing harder than coining proverbs every Sunday, or in playing revelational Guru week by week from your own philosophy or experience. It's tough enough letting God be God and trying to interpret what that means in a contemporary setting, without trying to be Abraham, Moses, Paul, and the Oracle of Delphi for Fifth Street Church.

Nobody invents the telephone for himself before making a call, but some men feel obligated to invent the whole religious world before breakfast every morning. Don't be ashamed to listen to the testimony of the Christian community of the past, both biblical and postbiblical witness. Others have already sought to interpret the biblical revelation. They can help. Hear them too.

Hold these textual ideas until maturity. Some of these biblical expressions will leap full grown into sermons. Most won't. Don't preach green sermons. Let the original intriguing idea develop as you turn it over in your mind. Sometimes this may take months.

A good program of biblical study will yield many ideas, however, most of which are not so obscure. Make a note card on each of these texts and your initial impressions about them, and keep them for future use. (Personally, for these textual idea cards, and illustrative material cards also, I prefer a very sophisticated filing system known as the "Messy Drawer Filing System"! Put a rubber band around them and drop them into a drawer. That's it. Go through them when you need them.)

Realistically, no contemporary preacher can spend months maturing every sermon idea. We must use more of a hothouse culture system. And if every sermon is not absolutely finished—and which one is?—give the congregation credit for being able to take a solid concept and work out the maturing of it in their own experience. But "be not deceived, God is not mocked," and neither is a contemporary church, by flashy phrases that are apparently profound and actually empty.

2. CONTEMPORARY SOURCES

Either the Bible or the contemporary situation may lead to sermons. Some preachers feel it is illegitimate to "get an idea and go find a text to match it." Not at all—providing that the idea has arisen from the need of people, and providing that the text is listened to once it is found. We must always be ready to be taught by the Word, or even to stand corrected by it if necessary. Our contemporary experience in Christ and the historic revelation of the Word must always be in dynamic interplay. In that sense, listening to the world about us also opens doors for sermonic thought, just as it did for Jesus in his earthy, practical, pictorial preaching.

Observe your environment. That's what Jesus did. Keep up. Study life. People. The news. Yourself. Be alert, aware, alive.

Stretch yourself. Get involved with a variety of interests. Don't preoccupy with your own tastes. Every church has both chess players and football fans. You don't have to be both, but you do have to appreciate both. "I am become all things . . ." (1 Cor. 9:22). That's why children wanted to listen to Jesus. No one has any trouble speaking to various age groups or special interest groups if he is interested in the interests of others, and shows it.

Develop a regular reading plan. No one can experience everything—and he shouldn't. Reading allows an extension of experience. Without it, don't ask why you have trouble finding ideas, or why you only preach "the same old things."

But where in the world do you start? Personally, I follow and recommend a six-fold reading plan, or "The Noble Six-fold Path to Reading." Rather than reading from one book one week and from another book another week, you will read wider and more satisfactorily if you read from six sources simultaneously.

Here's how it works. Select six books from six different categories of literature. Read a while from each book every week. Bracket those passages you want typed out. Drop in a note card at that page, and keep on reading. Type out these excerpts, or give the books to your secretary to type, once a week. Put the cards in a drawer and scan through the stack when sermon writing. They will speak for themselves to your specific needs. (I like this method better than indexing since one illustration can fit many topics. File or index these cards after preaching, either by topic or with the sermon itself.)

What are the six categories? They are arbitrary. Suit yourself. I would include novels; historical material (fiction and nonfiction); biography (such as *The Public Years*, Baruch; *From Pagan to Christian*, Lin Yutang); diaries and journals (*Markings*, Dag Hammerskjold; *Notebooks*, Camus; Whitefield and Wesley's *Journals*); poetry (separate volumes and anthologies; *One Hundred Modern Poems; A Treasury of Christian Verse*). The sixth I leave open for any miscellaneous work that comes to my attention. You may fill it with a special interest, such as drama or science. (Maybe it shouldn't be, but I consider it mandatory to schedule definite time for reading theology. Either add it as a category, or schedule a separate time to read those books and journals.)

When I finish a book in any category, I replace it with one of the same category. In that way my reading can be comprehensive and planned, yet varied. I read in any book I like, as long as I like.

A program of this sort will prove to be one of the most

rewarding things you can do. It will provide a practical way for the preacher to get the help literature can provide: aiding his understanding of life, in and of itself, which is primary; and serving as a communication tool to help others understand the Christian message.

How do I get from a text to a sermon? From an idea to a text?

This is the other tough question about starting a sermon. Assuming I've located a text, how do I get to a sermon? Or if I've got an idea, what do I do about the Bible?

It's the middle ground that kills us. That is, we have learned how to exegete texts, and likely also how to analyze contemporary psychological and ethical situations—but how do you get the two together? How do you move from one to the other? The process is really circular; so we could begin at either point, but I'll start with the traditional movement, text to sermon.

1. FROM TEXT TO SERMON

Assuming that the preacher knows how to study a biblical text, historically and critically, and that he is keenly aware of his contemporary setting for ministry, he may still have trouble. He may either use a text as a kind of underwriter's label of spiritual safety on a clever contemporary essay, or he may do a first-century travelogue on manners and customs of Bible lands. Depending on his training and theology, he may have trouble one way or another in authentically involving the Bible in the sermon.

Three suggestions may help us to move through the middle ground between the historical and the contemporary. Ask these questions of a text:

Where does God encounter the human situation in this text? What human issues, problems, and concerns are illumined by this passage? What does God reveal about our common lives in the ancient narrative? List every reason you can see for this word to have been retained as revelation: What does it tell us about ourselves? About one another? About God? What insights does it provide, what truths, about our specific contemporary situation? Determine the basic concern which strikes you from the text. The theme and structure of the sermon will eventually emerge from this inquiry.

What difference would it make if we all heard this word? How would life be affected if we all were willing to hear the word of this revelation? What changes would come to our lives if we would believe it, act on it? Listing these possible effects gives point and purpose to the sermon. They clearly establish the need for our specific human response to God's initiative.

What homiletical focuses are possible within this text? People, sayings, events, or the setting of the text itself? In the healing of the boy following the transfiguration (Mark 9:14–29), for example, a sermon might focus on one or more of the *people* involved: the boy, the father; the disciples; the crowd; Jesus. Or on the *sayings:* "Why could not we cast him out?" (9:28); "Lord, I believe, help thou mine unbelief" (9:24). Or on the *events:* the healing; the questioning of the scribes; the failure of the disciples. Or on the *setting:* the contrast of this experience following the transfiguration events.

Even if all of these elements were used in a sermon, one of them would likely provide the principal focus on the text and the remaining incidents would be a part of the peripheral vision of the sermon. And if only one or two verses out of the pericope actually form the actual text (*textus,* fabric) of the sermon, the remaining verses form the context.

When these three questions have been examined, the preacher has taken concrete steps in the middle ground—that is, practical hermeneutics—between text and today.

2. FROM IDEA TO TEXT

Obviously many of the sermons of Jesus arose from his encounters with people and their needs. The same will be true of any minister for Christ. Daily ministry and observation of life will call for Christian proclamation. Many of these ideas will readily identify with Scripture; some will not. What procedure is possible in these situations?

In all cases, exegete the basic principle underlying the contemporary situation. It is possible to preach on many subjects that have no specific biblical precedent; for example, the modern drug culture. If any contemporary issue is troubling or challenging to the life of the congregation—either immediately or ultimately—then analyze the life principle of the question. What is its basic issue? The accuracy of the pastor's exegesis of the contemporary scene in this case is a key to the worth of the sermon it produces; exactly, in fact, as sermons that begin from a text must correctly exegete the historical scene to be Christian proclamation.

Compare and contrast the contemporary approach to this principle with the Christian message. Several years ago I heard a sermon on the so-called "hippie" communities in California. The speaker identified their concept of love as the distinguishing principle of that culture and compared and contrasted the views of that group on love with the biblical principle. In this case, the sermon was actually about love, the text was on love, and the hippie experiment became a running illustration, pro and con, throughout the sermon.

Be careful to be fair both to the contemporary issue and to the text. Don't fight straw men. If you don't really have the facts on an issue, or if you can't be fair to it, then you are not ready to preach on it. Likewise, if you don't really intend to listen to the Bible when you get there, don't use it as a motto on your own personal battle flag. Cultural religion is always promoted by this abuse.

"And the Sermon Was Without Form and Void, and Darkness Was Upon the Face of the Deep"

A second cluster of practical questions surrounds the form of the sermon. How can the preacher find a procedure that implements the principles previously described? How do the traditional sermon parts relate to this theology of proclamation? Or do they?

All sermon preparation goes through three phases. In *phase one*, the sermon is without form and void and darkness is upon the face of the deep. This is the stage of creative chaos, but it is a necessary phase in sermon preparation.

In *phase two*, "let all things be done decently and in order." No sermon talks about everything, in just any fashion—or it shouldn't. The basic unity and movement of the sermon are established in this second phase. Simplicity, strength, and cleanness of design should typify the sermon at this stage.

But this is not the final step. Some preachers go into the pulpit in chaos, and others preach in neat, rigid structures, but neither is the proper final state of the sermon. *Phase three* involves making the sermon an oral product, something *sayable* —"and they listened the more willingly . . . " It is this phase that is most often neglected, and yet it is the one most readily apparent to the congregation. They know the sermon is an acoustic event, even if the preacher does not. For this reason, I have already stressed the necessity for oral preparation.

But what practical structural suggestions might facilitate this process?

Is an outline necessary, evil, or a necessary evil?

First, we must understand the difference between neoscholastic preaching and what we may refer to as gestaltic preaching. In neoscholastic preaching, "points" are overemphasized; the point gets lost in the points. In gestaltic preaching, the whole is greater than the sum of its parts. The *what* of the sermon, its message and mood, the whole dominates in gestaltic preaching. Some suggestions toward wholistic sermons:

1. Unity and movement are the only indispensable elements in structure. Outlines may help that, but only if they are natural rather than forced. Natural outlines are called forth by the material; forced outlines are superimposed on the material.

Nevertheless, in every case a sermon must have a basic unity of theme, or message, or mood if it is to be understood. (If you wish to communicate chaos or confusion as a message—for whatever reason—then disorder and non sequiturs are appropriate.) *Movement* is also essential. A sermon must start somewhere and go somewhere. "Points" are only ways of indicating movement.

If the whole of the theme must be divided for clarity, the parts must equal the whole. (Or, in other words, if you can't eat a whole apple in one bite, slice it into pieces; but the pieces, if put back together, must equal an apple, not a hybrid apple-lemon.) Otherwise, no unity is present and no movement is possible.

That is, if the whole message cannot be heard in one basic thematic statement which is first stated, then explained, described, and illustrated (as in a "one-point" sermon), then divide it into basic directional sentences ("points") which provide understandable movement for the theme.

2. Use no subdivisions at all. Subdivisions are a sure way to confusion and reflect an overemphasis on "points" and ideas. A "three-point" sermon, each with three subpoints, is a nine-point (idea) sermon. All a preacher can do with a sermon like that is talk himself to death trying to explain so many ideas.

I would suggest this as a basic rule: Only subdivide if forced to by the text. Do so only for textual clarity and fidelity, to set forth the basic concern of the text, never for random listing of additional explanatory ideas.

3. Allow the development within the sermon to proceed functionally. That is, allow the *explanation of the text* and the *statement of the human situation* to put flesh and blood on the bones of the key ideas.

In other words, in developing each of your basic idea-statements (divisions), you should deal with two functional elements: the *historical given* (declaration of the gospel; presentation of the historical revelation; explanation of the text), and with the *contemporary given* (description of the present situation; relation of the Scripture to contemporary life), rather than abstractly subdividing and subsubdividing thematic inferences which probably get away from both.

Do not rely upon endless subdividing of ideas, in neoscholastic fashion, to provide the content of the sermon. Many a preacher trained in this art has wound up with an elaborately complex outline and still had no idea what on earth to *say* once he stood up to speak.

Two principles may help this process:

(a) Remember that pictorial, illustrative material may help to clarify either of these functional elements. Use *alternative repetition:* alternate more abstract idea-language with picture language. People cannot listen long to theory without pictures that explain it. (Better yet, let the pictures come first and result in the theory.)

(b) Remember also another basic law: *Compaction increases density.* The more terse and epigrammatic your sentences, the greater their sectional density. Eventually they become steel-jacketed bullets that fire right through your audience with zero impact. (Another problem of a tightly written manuscript.)

4. Use transitional sentences to facilitate movement. These are linking sentences, sentences which move the sermon from one key thought to another. Between the introduction and the first division, a transitional sentence tells us that the whole concern of the sermon also involves a specific thought; between each of the divisions, a transitional sentence tells us that there is more to come.

There are three basic kinds of transitions, the fully stated, partly stated, and fully suggested transitional sentence:

(a) *Fully stated.* Both the previous idea and the subsequent idea are stated: "So the resurrection of Christ speaks of God's victory, but it also speaks of our victory." The formula for the fully stated transition is X, X: content on both sides of the link.

(b) *Partly stated.* Either the previous idea or the subsequent idea is stated, and the other suggested. Two formulas are possible: X, ?; or ?, X. Content is present on only one side of the equation. For example: "The resurrection of Christ speaks of God's victory, but is that all it says to us?" (X, ?.) Or, "This is one meaning of the resurrection; but it also speaks of our victory as well. (?, X.) In the first example, where we have been in the sermon is stated and where we are going is implied; in the second, where we have been is implied and where we are going is stated.

(c) *Fully suggested.* Neither the previous idea nor the subsequent one is stated; both are implied. The formula is ?, ?. No specific content is present at all. For example, "The resurrection assures us of one victory. But there is another." Or, quite simply, "But is that all?" In this case, "that" points backward, "all" points ahead.

How do we know which of these transitions to use? The oral manuscript itself will lead toward one or the other. For example, if a division closes explicitly with the key idea, then it would be ridiculous to immediately repeat that idea in a fully stated transitional sentence. Either a partly stated or fully suggested transition would better establish the unity and facilitate the movement of the sermon. But if a division has not explicitly stated its point, then a fully stated transition may be appropriate.

Oral practice will soon lead to logical and natural transitioning.

5. Remember that creative forms for sermon presentation result from sound principles.

Fosdick described his three basic forms as the box sermon (three points, or so, nailed up in parallel fashion like boards in a box—which form he said he liked least, but did most); the river sermon (one point, winding around many turns but staying within the banks of the same river); and the tree sermon (organic development, with growth and interrelationships shown: "it begins with this; it leads to this; it results in this").

Luccock described countless special forms: chase technique (idea pursued: "is it; is it; is it?"); classification sermon ("some do this; some do that; and others do thus and so"); ladder sermon (one idea builds upon another), etc. Contemporary homileticians have favored forms from the arts, use of varied media, talk-back styles, narrative forms (telling a story), and countless other creative innovations.

Which is best?

If a form suits the meaning and message of the sermon, if it follows meaningful methods appropriate to good theology of proclamation, and if it is the form which allows the historic revelation to speak most distinctly to its contemporary congregation—it is good structure, whatever its arrangement.

What about introductions, conclusions, titles?

At this point we are ready to deal with these traditional sermon parts. Obviously they have had a place in traditional homiletics. Are they essential to all sermon forms?

1. INTRODUCTIONS

Not all sermons must have introductions, but all sermons must begin. And however the sermon develops, the same two principles hold true for the beginning of every sermon: *It must be concrete rather than abstract; and it must plainly set the direction for the sermon.* I prefer to start with something that can be photographed—something tangible and tactile rather than abstract and theoretical. Begin as close to reality as language can manage. After all, we are speaking to people, not about subjects.

When is it appropriate to create an introduction in the traditional sense of a distinct sermon part? If the sermon has divisions, one is generally needed. Why? Because the congregation may become confused otherwise. They may lose the point in the points. They will not know what "point one" is a division of.

A traditional introduction typically does three things for the sermon: It reveals the basic concern of the message; it makes contact with the people; and it establishes contact with the Word. (I say "typically," because the direct use of a text, for example, may not occur in the introduction, though it frequently will.) That is, an introduction will *create interest for the theme from the text.* These three elements are on a lateral plane; each arises out of and relates to the other. They may occur in any order.

But it is important that every sermon begin *concretely, spe-*

cifically, rather than theoretically or abstractly. If the text is a graphic, colorful narrative, the sermon may well open with it. But if it is a weighty, difficult Pauline section, for example, or an obscure bit of Hebrew history, then perhaps the sermon should begin with a description of events in the contemporary situation that will arouse interest in the text. Try some arrangement of these elements aloud; revise it if it doesn't provide the necessary unity and movement.

Regardless of which comes where, however, be sure that the beginning of the sermon plainly reveals the concern of the sermon, the theme of the sermon, the *what* of the sermon; and that it arouses interest in that, rather than in one of the lesser divisions of the sermon.

A frequent fault is using the introduction to introduce the first point rather than the whole of the sermon. Another mistake is failing to subordinate interest-arousing material to the concern of the sermon as a whole, so that the congregation may be quite interested in some colorful piece of material but is distracted from, rather than attracted to, the larger purpose of the message.

May a sermon do without an introduction? (Barth would ask if one *may* have an introduction.) Definitely. If the order of the sermon as a whole proceeds functionally—that is, without idea-divisions at all—then a formal introduction is not required. The sermon simply unfolds inductively, explaining and applying its single, undivided concern as it proceeds.

2. CONCLUSIONS

The same which has been said about introductions may also be said for the conclusion of the sermon. Not all sermons have conclusions, but all sermons must conclude. Like the introduction, the conclusion must be specific and pointed rather than vague and abstract. With or without a formal conclusion, this principle holds true for the end of the sermon.

If the final division of the sermon has brought the message to a conclusive climax, tacking on a formal part called a conclusion is pointless. But if it is important to the message to tie together the lines of thought that have been opened, an explicit conclusion can make plain the concern of the sermon. This may be done by summary, challenge, or appeal.

3. TITLES

A subject and a title are not the same. A subject is what the sermon is about; a title is what you call it. Titles are not really very important. Relatively speaking. A good one creates interest and helps make specific the subject. But no one should make a fetish out of catchy title-building.

After all, how can a title really be used? In the newspaper, church program, billboard? Perhaps. If a title is used in the sermon itself, it must be introduced naturally; that is, said in a normal sentence. Not, "If I had a title today, I suppose I should call it . . ." Of course you've got one—otherwise, you wouldn't be saying that in the first place! If it can't be said naturally, forget it.

Titles traditionally have been classified as descriptive or poetic; more analytic, or more suggestive. But any title should do some of both: indicate the sermon direction, and arouse interest. Titles may take the form of sentences, questions, exclamations, or phrases with limiting or descriptive words. One rule: When in doubt, don't. That is, use good taste; and be plain rather than strange.

Of Time and the River

The final practical question concerning sermon building is in some ways the most important one. How do I do it? What kind of a schedule will allow me to do my other work and still preach effectively? Must I obey Fosdick's Law: an hour in the study for each minute in the pulpit? (Or shall I resign now?)

How do I do it?

Naturally nobody can set up a weekly schedule for anyone else. There are a few principles that may help:

1. Forget about "an hour for a minute." That is a contemporary impossibility. Some of us preach two or three times a week. (Like it or not!) And anyway, that would give a disproportionate place to sermons in the total task of ministry. If you can allocate fifteen solid hours a week to the preparation of the total sermon and Bible-teaching duties, you're doing well. And that's an outside figure. (I'm not counting every possible minute at home or on the street that the sermon may be working in your mind.)

2. Try to reserve morning for study. At least, all but the last hour (11:00 A.M.–12:00 noon). Realistically, you will have to return calls, answer mail, hold conferences. But try to guard the fresh hours for mind work. Start early. Use afternoons for outside calling, hospital ministries, etc.

3. Arrange the week to help the process. Monday ought to be Low Motivation day (if you work at all). Do whatever does not call for the highest motivation. Traditionally, preachers haven't exactly raced into next Sunday's sermon on Monday. (If you can, congratulations. Your prize is on the way.)

Personally, I arrange my sermonic week this way: Monday is my morning for reading (do something else if that kills you to think about it); Tuesday I do devotional study, preliminary exegesis, and attempt a tentative sermon structure; Wednesday I do Bible study (from one Old Testament and one New Testament book; one feeds my midweek Bible study, the other my Sunday evening sermon); Thursday I do my first oral manuscript; Friday I do my final oral manuscript, or Saturday, depending on time demands; and on one or the other, I complete my Sunday night oral preparation. (I try to do homilies, or Bible studies, on Sunday night to provide variety in worship and simplicity of sermon preparation. It also seems to suit the mood of the hour better.)

Arrange the week to suit your own needs. But recognize the limitations on your time, get started early (in the day, and in the week), and keep up your contact with the Bible and with contemporary life.

How far ahead should I plan? And how?

Some men can work out a year's plan in advance, complete with titles and texts. They don't need my help. I need theirs.

I do believe that planning as specifically as that a quarter ahead is good. In my opinion, however, a general, open plan for a full year is more helpful. Here are some principles:

1. Block off on a calendar all holidays and church holy days (Christmas, Easter, etc.). Plan to preach sermons that will deal with these high days, or perhaps series to lead up to them.

2. Select *some* local and denominational church emphases to be observed (Christian Home Week, Mission Week, Stewardship Sunday, etc., etc.—you couldn't preach on all of them unless you spent all day at church every Sunday).

3. For the remaining weeks, indicate month by month (more or less), portions of the Bible to be covered, sermon objectives to be pursued (devotional sermons, ethical themes, etc.), special sermon types to be used (biographical, dialogue, life-situational, etc.), or sermon series to be followed (the Lord's Prayer, the Ten Commandments, etc.). These may be indicated on the calendar singularly or in combination.

For example, in the first quarter of the year you might choose to preach from the minor Prophets and the pastoral Epistles; or, in the evenings, devotional sermons from the Psalms; in the second quarter, ethical messages on the home and family for several weeks, and dialogue sessions in the evenings on the morning sermons. And so on. Endless permutations and combinations of these very general, basic elements are possible and provide at least some security and comprehensiveness in your preaching program.

4. At any rate, try to set out a plan that will help you, not get in your way or become artificial. Change it if you need to; never let it interfere with a real need. A good general plan, however, will prove useful by preventing monochromatic preaching and pet-theme pursuit, and by promoting broad use of the Scripture and a variety of approaches.

At this point, it's every man for himself. Perhaps one man's approach-for-now may have helped to add an idea or so to someone else's personal program. I hope so. If not, don't complain; send help.

Because of the essential place of language in this whole approach to sermon building and presentation, we must now shift our attention to that crucial area, to its proper use, and to its perversion.

10

"SOME SAID IT THUNDERED": UPPER GARBLE AND LOWER GARBLE

Perhaps it is some primitive appendage, a kind of religious appendix, that causes men to continue to confuse thunder with the divine voice. When the voice from heaven spoke to Jesus shortly before his last Passover, a voice which Jesus explicitly said "came not because of me, but for your sakes," the people who stood by and heard it "said that it thundered: others said, an angel spoke to him" (John 12:23–30).

Unfortunately that misunderstanding is not an isolated phenomenon. It happens every Sunday, somewhere, for both preachers and laymen. The occasional church visitor and perpetual pew-sitter alike have great difficulty in identifying the Word among so many words. What does the true voice from God sound like?

That question also haunts the preacher, afflicted on the one hand with the uneasy suspicion that he is human and on the other hand with the uncomfortable assignment of believing that somehow God can speak the Word through his mouth. Unless his approach to preaching is fully incarnational, his speech will betray him worse than that of Simon Peter in the courtyard.

The preacher's futile attempts to sound less like himself and more like God may take one of two directions. He may alter his own speech into a more authoritarian, hence more thunderous, tone in an effort to sound more self-assured and therefore less vulnerable. After all, what layman would be impressed if he used his own normal, often-fallible voice in the pulpit? ("Do we not know this man? Is he not the carpenter's son?") There must be a kind of *ex-cathedra* ring to it if anyone is to imagine that God is somehow speaking through it. Or else he may seek the more elegant, high-flown speech of the celestial regions, complete with the faintest suggestion of a rustling of angel's wings in the background. Invariably these attempts impress people as either meaningless noise or less than human verbalism. In neither case, however, is the word of God recognized.

That is not to say that these efforts are without results. They obviously impress somebody favorably or they would not go on. The fact is, they are largely, although not exclusively, the result of the demands of the laity. The layman must share the blame for the artificiality of pulpit speech. It is true that the young preacher often cultivates these accents as a kind of ministerial union card. But it is equally true that many an otherwise human young man has been driven into unnatural speech because of the insistence that "our preacher should sound like a preacher." Which means, of course, that he is to sound holy; that he is to sound different in order to be respected.

This is another chicken-and-egg syndrome: generations of preachers have gotten by, if not succeeded, by using the tone which the congregation recognizes as "religious," which in turn conditions another generation of laymen to what pulpit speech ought to sound like. Who started what is not important. *The continuing lack of faith on the part of both preachers and laymen alike that God can and will speak through normal human beings is to blame.*

Actually there are two reasons for the remote dialects of the pulpit, although both are only opposite sides of the same fault. The first is this desire for quasi-divine speech, this preoccupation of both layman and preacher with the search for the divine note which will unmistakably be perceived as heavenly. But the second is like unto it—in fact, it is difficult to imagine that the first could have occurred without it—the isolation of the pulpit.

Isolation breeds dialect. The more isolated the region, the more obscure the dialect. And if the isolation is acute enough, another language emerges. This is true of remote island peoples and primitive jungle tribes with their unique languages, but it is equally true of isolated sections of advanced nations such as the United States or Germany. (Even today in Germany, for example, there are villages no more than two miles apart where the inhabitants can instantly recognize one another due to a peculiar tone on one sound or another.)

There is a certain romance to dialect, a certain nostalgia at its passing. There is presently a kind of speech-ecology movement dedicated to protecting the uniqueness of dialect and to preventing its falling victim to speech generalization, an effort which is closely akin to preserving the ivory-billed woodpecker or the whooping crane. Accents add variety and color to life; they may be quaint, or even amusing. But there is a less than funny side to dialect also, as when it hinders or absolutely blocks communication, or when it causes bitter sectionalism and thereby isolates and separates human beings from true community.

The pulpit, like all isolated regions, has its own peculiar dialects. Likewise, it has suffered from all of the problems associated with dialect-separation. This separation of the pulpit is not primarily a geographical or spatial isolation, though that plays some role. There are two sources of pulpit separation, and each has produced its own distinctive dialect.

The first of these is *attitudinal separation,* an isolation consciously or unconsciously chosen by the provincial preacher, the man who is provincial because of his remoteness either to the world or to the Word. It is equally as provincial to ignore the significance of the Word as to ignore the significance of the world. The truest mark of provincialism is still that of loving "every age but this and every culture but your own," in the words of Gilbert and Sullivan .This means that the most sophisticated and spatially involved preacher may be as provincial, and therefore as dialect-separated, as the most geographically or sectarially isolated preacher.

Both "liberal" and "fundamentalist" wings of the church are equal jargon-users. Too intense preoccupation with the historical given produces cultic speech; too intense preoccupation with the existential given produces ultimately meaningless speech. Only midpoint, incarnational preaching, produces speech that is truly intelligible.

But dialect-separation may also exist where there is no serious attitudinal problem on the part of the preacher, but where a *methodological breakdown* has occurred. This is the second source of pulpit separation. As, for example, where a preacher struggles helplessly to escape the nonspeech of pulpit dialect but cannot because he simply does not know what it is in his language or method that is isolating him. Here the problem is not primarily due to disjointed theology of proclamation, but to faulty technique in preaching.

Thus the pulpit has produced two distinct dialects: *Upper Garble* and *Lower Garble*. Upper Garble is that dialect produced by attitudinal separation; Lower Garble results from faulty technique. Of course neither of these dialects is entirely independent of either attitude or technique, but at least the two are sufficiently distinct as to be described. Perhaps it would be interesting to note the principles for these two varieties of pulpit dialect, Upper Garble and Lower Garble.

Upper Garble

1. *Never uses a short word when a long one would be more impressive.* This is the key to Upper Garble: impressiveness. Language can conceal as well as reveal. When the preacher does not feel sufficiently impressive, Upper Garble can compensate for his insecurity. Short words can be used on every street corner; lengthy words are more complex and therefore more suggestive of the mysterious, the more-than-human, the

profound. Upper Garble users seem never to notice that Jesus spoke simply.

Jacques Barzun illustrates this desire for impressiveness which statesmen, who must never appear mortal or fallible, seem to share in common with preachers: "A single word gives us away, as when President Eisenhower said: 'Marshall Zhukov and I *operated* together very closely' (*New York Times*, July 18, 1957). Not *worked*—'operated.' Why 'operated'? Because it is loftier, more abstract, more suggestive of complex doings, more praiseworthy because more pretentious—one senses the careful effort that goes into operating closely together. And when a plain, straightforward army man falls unknowingly into pretentiousness, one can gauge how powerful the cultural pressure is to be a pedant."[1]

Even the simplest expressions can be rendered unintelligible: "A mass of concentrated earthly material perennially rotating on its axis will not accumulate an accretion of bryophytic vegetation. (A rolling stone gathers no moss.) That prudent *Aves* which matutinally deserts the cosiness of its abode will ensnare a vermiform creature. (The early bird catches the worm.) Aberration is the hallmark of homo sapiens while longanimous placability and condonation are the indicia of supramundane omniscience. (To err is human, to forgive, divine.)"[2]

The basic fault of Upper Garble is not that it can only be understood by intellectuals and therefore has a limited audience. Its real error is that it does not say sharply what it means, which opens it to the question of whether it *understands* sharply what it means. "What this theology explicates. . ." "Explicates" is like bringing an aardvark into the room and asking who knows what it is; or better, it is like shoving an empty trunk into the room and asking who knows what's in it.

Through long years of careful practice, the user of Upper Garble can systematically replace every short word in his vocabulary with a longer one which will be more difficult to understand. With a little luck, he may get so obscure that no one will confuse him with a human being.

2. *Always uses theo-philosophic language.* Every vocation

has its professional jargon and its professional manner. The doctor does, as he sweeps through hospital corridors trailed by his entourage of nurses and interns, pausing briefly to "explain" a medical situation in terms that often leave the patient or family more confused than before; so does the counseling psychologist whose manner of speech has become so nondirective and clinical that it has the sound of a man tiptoeing on eggshells.

Both vocabulary and manner are the carefully cultivated practices of the ages, and they are especially employed by those who are often expected to do the impossible and are unwilling to face the reality of their own humanity and fallibility.

Theology has a long head start in this respect over all other professions. Its professional jargon is multicenturies old and is not merely hidden in the mysteries of the complex workings of the body or the mind, but the "soul." Therefore it has more at stake. The expertness of the theological specialist cannot be as easily established as that of a surgeon through a successful operation, or that of a psychologist through a successful counseling experience. He has no licensing board to prevent other Christians from practicing theology as doctors do to prevent laymen from practicing medicine. Religion is like politics: Everybody is an expert.

As a result, the preacher has a particularly hard time maintaining his authority. He may be tempted to use obscure jargon to prove his expertness.

The professional training of any specialist is a process of encoding; that is, an input into his mind of technical terms useful to his specialty. There is nothing basically wrong with that. It is necessary to facilitate technical communication between specialists. But problems develop when an encoded specialist tries to communicate without decoding his information. Then the person who has not had the benefit of encoding is bewildered, if somewhat impressed. This kind of encoded communication is perfectly understandable among fellow specialists, even if it is cryptic to outsiders. That is the reason two theologians in conversation resemble nothing so much as two computers talking to one another. But if the computer wants to talk to human beings, it must use a language people can understand.

The preacher, who is trained by theologians and similarly encoded, can never quite escape the mysterious glamour of the complex world of the theological laboratory. Even though he must talk to laymen, mere "commoners" in the art of theological speech, he is tempted to show the lofty region of his training by his dialect. He wants to prove to a world of secular godlings—doctors, scientific types, insurance underwriters—that he is *too* a specialist. So he pulls out all the stops. He speaks of surd evil and patripassionism; he quotes obscure theologians and cites the proceedings of ancient church councils; he drops what few Greek and Hebrew phrases he remembers.

By doing so, he gets the best of both worlds. His credibility is high as a fully accredited scientific specialist whose long years of technical training are obviously in evidence, and his knowledge of the mysterious God he purports to represent is safely cloaked under a cloud of obscurity which the layman can admire if he cannot understand.

That attitude is typified by the old woman who came out of church shaking her head in wonderment and saying, "Our pastor must be a smart man—we can't understand a word he says!"

That preacher only made one mistake, and so did the old woman: They both confused obscurity with profundity. Jesus was profound, never obscure. He had profound thoughts and simple language. We are just the opposite: We have profound language and simple thoughts. In Spurgeon's lectures to his students, he once told them that preachers who were admired for being "deep" reminded him of a well: "You look down into a well, if it be empty it will appear to be very deep, but if there be water in it you will see its brightness. I believe that many 'deep' preachers are simply so because they are like dry wells with nothing whatever in them, except decaying leaves, a few stones, and perhaps a dead cat or two."[3]

3. *Strives for elevated or inflated language.* Polysyllabic
language, theo-philosophic language, and inflated language
are three different means of sounding impressive. Polysyllabic
language is impressive simply because it uses big words (like
"polysyllabic"). Theo-philosophic language is impressive
because it is the exclusive property of the theological specialist. But inflated language has its own special function. Through
a careful use of adjectives, the most ordinary event can be
turned into a spectacle. That is particularly useful to the
preacher who does not want his parishioners to mistake the
noble realm of the religious world with everyday life.

For example, everything must become "marvelous," "won-
derful," "glorious." By connecting his ministerial air-hose, the
preacher of Upper Garble can inflate the simplest and most
solid words into swollen, great bloated things to be released
and go floating out over the heads of a gaping congregation. If
the choir sang well, it was "glorious." If the last meeting of the
deacons or elders concluded without a fistfight, it was "won-
derful" (that may not be overly inflated!).

This language is particularly useful among preachers. For
example, if questioned about last Sunday's services, the upper-
garbling preacher can reply, "Marvelous!"—when what he
really means is, "Mediocre." (Actually, the only thing "marvelous" about the service is that there was anybody there at all!)

The effect of these words is even more enhanced when they
themselves are inflated by prolonging the initial vowel, as in
"maarvelous," "wuunderful," and "gloorious." A particularly
pious sound can be rendered by giving the same treatment to
the name of Jesus—"Jeesus." The longer, the holier. Similar
tricks can be played with consonants, too, for some reason long
lost in the archives of Upper Garble; as "Holy Spidit," for
"Holy Spirit," as though one had extreme nasal blockage.

Many a staunchly evangelical preacher who would never
turn his collar around backward has compensated for his lack
of clerical identification by turning his voice around backward.

At first, of course, this kind of speech is only laughable, if a
little pathetic. Young people, for example, usually snicker at

the spectacle of Brother Puffing-Adder or Reverend Blowfish. But there must be something addicting about it, because if fed on a steady diet of verbal soufflé the teeth of a congregation become unable to chew anything more substantial, and its taste seems to run to nothing else.

Unfortunately, however, such inflated language, like inflated currency, eventually becomes worthless. Nobody wants it; it is even hard to give away.

4. *Employs the grand manner.* The preacher who has become adept at the use of such elegant and complex language could scarcely be expected to act normally. He must find a manner to match his speech. His gestures, his expressions, his platform manner, his bearing, all must match his language.

Depending on his theological persuasion, this usually takes one of two courses: either he becomes Elizabethan, or Cool ("Cool" being defined as whatever is acceptable in those sophisticated in-circles that have rejected the out-circles; usually a carefully studied under-playing of the role). There are avid collectors of either manner, quite parallel to taste in furniture, either antique or modern.

For example, if a preacher is the usual old-style upper-garbler, one who prefers pious tones with matching theology, one whose rumbling basso or penetrating tenor energetically inflates words into grandiose proportions, then he is likely to be Elizabethan in style. He needs an immense stage to be displayed upon in order to be viewed in proper proportion. As one layman described his pastor, he seemed "too big for any one room." The effect is overwhelming: Large of gesture, expansive in warmth (sometimes also in girth), he resembles a ministerial Falstaff. Arms akimbo, arms crossed; fingers stabbing the heavens; head cocked; face in a scowl, now beaming like the sun; lips drawn back in a passable imitation of a smile; posturing and posing, gesticulating and declaiming. His vocabulary is even more archaic, dating back to Beowulf or the Venerable Bede.

This Elizabethan manner is quite adaptive, too, suiting many locales and confessional situations. The traditionalist of almost any denomination can employ it anywhere. It is equally at home in the pulpit of an elegant cathedral where it is polished for upper-class tastes, or in a rural backwoods setting where it is energetically pursued by the typical back-slapping, chicken-chomping, ice-box raiding, old-style parson. The benign paternalism which it conveys is equally appreciated by the insecure, authority-needing church member at either end of the social spectrum.

On the other hand, if the preacher is an avant-garde upper-garbler—and there are at least as many of those as traditionalists—his manner will be Cool rather than Elizabethan. But he is no less impressive, no less elegant. Every movement speaks of sophistication, of poise, of casual correctness. His awesome awareness of contemporary "in-ness" is no less intimidating than the ancient authoritarianism of the traditionalist. His expression is serene, almost guru-like, rather than bluff and hearty. Only traces of emotion show—most noticeably, perhaps, when denouncing emotion. He projects an indefinable air of sexiness along with his nonchalance and urbanity. His total manner is carefully calculated to keep him at the front of nondirective churchly fashion, the leader of those who cannot be led.

Perhaps the two are not really centuries apart in approach. After all, the world has never known an era of more elegant dandies and culture-conscious sophisticates than the Elizabethan age.

5. *Prizes involved reasoning.* There are times, even for the accomplished practicioner of Upper Garble, when the most naive parishioners begin to see through his language and manner. Then it is necessary to lose them in the dark woods of complex reasoning. If they cannot follow the tracks of inference and deduction no matter how carefully they trace the intricate patterns, then the mystery is safe and the authority of the upper-garbler is secure.

Plainness is one virtue that Upper Garble shuns like the plague. Nothing is more humiliating than being understood. (Particularly if what is said is meaningless.)

But by going around in endless logic-circles, even the most attentive hearer can be thrown off the track. At last he will give up the chase and go mentally home, baffled and fatigued, perhaps even irritated, but still impressed that something profound has been said which he somehow missed. How long, of course, he will continue to follow the hounds at the Sunday hunt is open to question. From the persistently declining attendance at worship, it is apparent that many people have already enjoyed all of the sport they can stand.

Nevertheless, the use of involved reasoning is a tested and true method of remaining impressive, particularly if administered in small doses, and should be mastered by every user of Upper Garble. As long ago as 1883, Austin Phelps described the practice in his classic work, *English Style in Public Discourse,* as he told of a German philosopher who rewrote part of a manuscript because he found it understandable.[4] With its long and impressive history, the device should not be overlooked.

6. *Overstates when confused.* Closely akin to the use of involved reasoning is the practice of overstating when confused. No one could be expected to be right *all* of the time, but superiority is difficult to maintain in the presence of error. It smacks too much of humanity. And infallibility is impossible.

The Bible has the unfortunate habit of putting the preacher into waters over his head. What is he to do then? Admit that he faces a truth he cannot understand? Confess that there are spiritual realities which he has not yet experienced? And thereby admit that he is only one very human Christian among others?

Not likely! Better to overstate, to explain everything, to eliminate paradox, to claim divine insight, to allude to personal spiritual triumphs. The more emphatically said, the better. A bit of verse expresses it well: "When in danger or in doubt, run in circles, scream and shout."

Helmut Thielicke warns against this kind of arrogance on the part of the minister. The preacher must confess his helplessness at certain points in interpreting the word of God. He must

confess that there are truths which are still beyond him, and yet
be able to point both himself and others to them. He can speak
of these truths—indeed, he must—he is bound to the whole
truth of Scripture, even those parts which he has not yet
experienced as a certainty in his own life and thought.

But he must not exaggerate; he must acknowledge without
shame those truths he is still waiting to apprehend and confess
them as expected truths. Then the preacher testifies that the
truth of the Scripture is greater than his own experience or
understanding. "But woe to him who acts as if he already 'saw'
all things, as if everything were equally clear to him, as if he
were looking without blinking into the thousand-watt lamp of
the whole truth."[5]

But such an approach requires humility, and humility is the
essence of the incarnational experience. Unless he is willing to
make that kind of sacrifice, the preacher would do better to
practice Upper Garble.

7. *Loses its humanity in its divinity.* Upper Garble is guilty of
homiletical Docetism. The preacher who practices it imagines
that his humanity is an illusion, that his spiritual nature alone
is real. That is heresy. The effects of this modern Docetic error
are far more widespread and deadly than its ancient counter-
part. It is no minor problem, no insignificeant misuse of elocution, no matter how comical certain aspects of it. Upper Garble
is a serious symtom of a deeply underlying problem, an indica-
tor of an acute spiritual sickness. It is the outward expression of
an inner disorder which can only lead to an abnormal existence
for both preacher and congregation.

This final principle of Upper Garble is actually not a separate
characteristic. It is rather a summary of the total error involved
in the dialect. This fault results from a false concept of authority, an insecurity on the part of the preacher which feeds on the
insecurities of the congregation. It is marked by an almost total
absence of genuine humanity in language and style.

This preacher has failed to grasp the essential humility
required of the servant of God. He has failed to notice that Jesus
himself took on the form of a man in his incarnation and

humbled himself in order to communicate and become one with men. We still need to be reminded that "the servant is not greater than his lord" (John 13:16). Jesus constantly struggled to conceal sufficiently his messianic nature so that he would not force a warped obedience on men. This struggle is reversed with the insecure preacher; instead of a "messianic secret," he is involved in a "human secret" in an effort to gain authority by concealing his weakness.

There is a distinct risk involved in humanity. Perhaps the preacher who attempts to conceal his humanity in Upper Garble once had his authority severely challenged and was so frightened and intimidated that he decided, perhaps unconsciously, that it was far safer to rise a step above the human.

But with no common ground under his feet, with no dust upon his shoes, the preacher cannot walk and talk with men. He is as safe, and as isolated, as a Greek god. And as unreal.

Lower Garble

Lower Garble is not free of attitudinal problems, of sins of the spirit, but basically this dialect is caused by faulty technique. The most humble and authentic preacher can still have great difficulty in projecting his genuine humanity as he proclaims the gospel. If he does, he may unconsciously suffer from one or more of the technical errors of Lower Garble that separate the pulpit from the Word or the world.

1. *Locates the sermon in ancient history.* This fault particularly plagues the preacher who attempts to be "biblical" in his preaching. His very concern to be faithful to the text may cause him to do little more than deliver a first-century history lecture. He becomes lost in Canaan and never finds his way into the twentieth century. He is almost totally preoccupied with ancient grammar, historical footnoting, and background studies.

It was most certainly a Lower Garbler about whom Fosdick wrote, "Only the preacher proceeds still upon the idea that folk

come to church desperately anxious to discover what happened to the Jebusites."[6] It is good to visit Canaan, but too
many preachers enter the pulpit carrying waterpots on their
heads.

Nevertheless, background studies and historical information
are essential to a correct interpretation of the biblical text.
Otherwise the significance of the text may be totally lost when
isolated from its historical context. Without a historical and
critical understanding of the Scripture, the sermon invariably
degenerates into a mere subjective discourse on whatever the
preacher himself particularly wants to say. But this historical
data itself cannot become the exclusive *focus* of the sermon.

Original language studies are also basic to an understanding
of the Scripture. Bonhoeffer said, "No sermon should be produced without use of the original text."[7] But if the preacher
uses Greek and Hebrew words in the pulpit, whether to demonstrate his expertness or simply as a misguided attempt to
"clarify" a difficult text, he has missed the point. Charles R.
Brown wrote, "The expository sermon is a product of exegesis,
but not an exhibition of it. It is altogether wise to dig beforehand with your Greek spade and your Hebrew shovel but not to
be digging while you are preaching."[8]

The results of original language exegesis and word studies
should be brought into the pulpit, but the tools should be left in
the study. Instead of saying, "The words *agape* and *phileo* are
two different Greek words for love," it is better to say, "The
New Testament describes love in two ways," and then describe
it. The point is to communicate the biblical concept, not to
display knowledge. Even when innocently done, the practice is
distracting and confusing and often opens the motivations of
the preacher to suspicion.

But if the sermon is not to wander around longer in the
historical wilderness than the Israelites trying to find the Promised Land, the cure of this malady is also not to reduce the
sermon to the six o'clock news report. The total absence of the
historical is as great a fault as preoccupation with it. Man
simply needs more than the time, the weather, and a vaguely
religious commentary upon the headlines.

Fosdick himself balanced his criticism of historical preoccupation with this remark: "If people do not come to church anxious about what happened to the Jebusites, neither do they come yearning to hear a lecturer express his personal opinion on themes which editors, columnists, and radio commentators have been dealing with throughout the week."[9]

2. *Speaks to no one in particular about nothing in particular.* The motto of this kind of preaching is, "I shot a sermon in the air, it fell to earth, I know not where." The title of some sermons could be, "Some Good Things to Do," or "And Another Thing . . . !"

Lower Garble suffers from an incurable vagueness. It speaks about man, not to men. It cannot clearly focus its eyes upon any one object. Every sermon is a hopeless collection of religious generalizations. No matter what text is chosen or what topic is announced, the course of the sermon eventually meanders around the same geography.

This kind of preaching is usually caused by a limited and preconceived notion of what the gospel really is. The Lower Garble preacher really has only one sermon, or at most two, which his prior insights have strongly impressed upon him. This previous experience has so programmed him that when his preaching button is pressed, the congregation hears the same prerecorded message. The preacher himself may be dimly aware of this limitation and may even struggle feebly against it for awhile, but eventually he gives up and resorts to a mere shuffling of illustrations, titles, and texts to provide a spurious variety in his preaching.

Almost every Christian has one or two sermons which his own experiences in the faith have yielded, but this subjective base is far too narrow for balanced Christian proclamation. The preacher must keep both the biblical and the contemporary in sharp focus, or else he will aimlessly cross the same dull terrain, having neither a specific message nor a specific party to deliver it to. He must pay more attention to what the Bible and the people are trying to tell him. In short, he needs to listen more and talk less.

Some preachers excuse their endless generalizations by in-

sisting that more specific preaching misses too many people.
The general theory seems to be that by shooting at nothing you
can hit everything. They are afraid that no one in the immediate audience may identify with a specific situation from either
the Bible or contemporary life.

But a person does not need to have suffered the loss of a
brother to identify with the grief of Mary and Martha, or the
pain of a runaway son to identify with the waiting father. In
both cases, however, these specifics are more tangible than
vague assurances murmured in the general direction of grief.
Everyone has suffered loss and known grief, and anyone can
and will immediately translate a specific grief situation into
applicable terms for his own experience. Then the Scripture's
assurance becomes his assurance, the biblical hope becomes
his hope. Otherwise the gospel remains a historical abstraction
not spoken to him; the sermon, a pointless arrow fired into
midair.

3. *Lacks vividness because it never becomes involved.* Closely related to generalized preaching, and yet distinct from it,
is uninvolved preaching. Much preaching is vague and generalized because the preacher is personally uninvolved. This
does not mean that he does not tell enough personal illustrations, or that he should establish the gospel on the basis of his
own experiences. It means two things: First, that his preaching
lacks perspective; and second, that it focuses on subjects rather
than on people, that it is third-person preaching.

As Helmut Thielicke has pointed out, vividness is a matter of
perspective. For example, a trip through the mountains is
exciting, crossing a plain is dull and uninteresting. The difference is that the mountains provide a changing perspective, the
plain is constantly flat. Unless the preacher often positionizes
himself and his audience relative to issues and to life, listening
to his sermon will be like driving for hours through Kansas
wheat fields or across Texas plains, hoping every moment to
see some hill or tree stick up on the horizon to break the
monotony of the landscape.

Thielicke says: "Perspective means that what I see and what I communicate to others is related to the observer's standpoint and that it always communicates my relationship to things too. . . . You have no 'perspective' in your theology; it is all flat. And that means, first, that there is no distinction between what is nearer and what is more remote, between what is primary and what is secondary, and so there is no focal point; and second, you do not reveal your own relationship or attitude to these things, that is, you do not emerge as perspective center. And the result is that there is no vividness."[10]

There is also no reality, and often no honesty. The preacher must be willing to take a true stance, his own stance with reference to the issues of life. Every stance will gain a following anyhow. The preacher might as well pick the one that is truly his—he may have to live with it for a long time.

Without perspective, everything is distorted. Unless the preacher honestly positionizes himself and the doctrines he preaches relative to the Bible and to life, mountains become molehills and an ordinary man becomes a spiritual giant. He must not appear to stand equidistant to all spiritual reality.

This does not mean that he is to be forever parading his spiritual shortcomings or his theological confusion, or that he is to join an honesty cult. It does mean that he is not to make every biblical admonition sound equally easy, and that he does not have to pretend to understand everything in the Bible or to have accomplished every spiritual challenge.

Nor is it necessary to say, "I never pray for others, but you should." Honesty only demands that a true perspective be given: "Praying for others is not easy. At least not for me, and perhaps not for you either." Rather than lowering his credibility, this kind of perspective-preaching gives the preacher believability and the sermon a great increase in vividness.

Lower Garble also lacks vividness because it is always talking about "it," never about "you" and "me." Again, this is not a question of application, but of focus. In Lower Garble, the subject of the sermon is its subject, not its hearers. That may seem logical enough, but it is a great fault. Of course the sermon must have a unifying concern, and the preacher ought to stick to it and not preach all over the known world. But if he *focuses* on his subject instead of on the people for whom the message of the gospel is intended, he begins to monologue with himself. He becomes infatuated with ideas and may be guilty of theme-worship.

It is as though the preacher turned ninety degrees away from the audience to address his subject. If the audience likes, it may look at the subject with him. But only he and his subject are in dialogue; the hearers are passive spectators. The preacher is like a juggler of colored balls; his ideas are the balls, and his total concentration is required to keep them all up in the air at the same time. A few years of this kind of preoccupied preaching, and the whole congregation could get up and silently tiptoe out without his ever missing them.

A congregation, however, long accustomed to the role of mere passive observer, usually resents more active involvement and contents itself with merely applauding good performances: "Doesn't he do it *well?* Doesn't our preacher do it as well as anybody you've ever *seen?*" *What* he is doing, of course, is another question. And this kind of performing, more than anything else, is responsible for the generations of pew-critics who regard their sole business in church as that of being entertained and of passing sour-faced judgments on poor performances.

This third-person, "it"-centered preaching removes vividness from the sermon because the congregation is not involved. It fosters an impersonal attitude on the part of both preacher and congregation which promotes oratory rather than conversation. It deceives the congregation into believing that the worship hour, or at least the preached part of it, is a time for the passive observation of an oratorical performance which takes place external to them, and largely external to the preacher. (The effect is heightened if he reads a manuscript.)

At best it is briefly entertaining, at worst, deadly dull. But whatever it is, the sermon is never a vital, living encounter between God and his people.

4. *Lacks imagination totally.* This is the chief creative error of Lower Garble. It is marked by obvious words, ordinary ideas,

and predictable order. Lower Garble is "ho-hum" preaching. It may avoid the rococo speech of Upper Garble with its endless flourishes and fretwork, but its own blockhouse style is scarcely an improvement.

To begin with, its words are obvious. A word does not need to be long, or technical, or inflated to avoid the obvious. It can simply be fresh, vivid, angular, tactile. With thought, the simplest words can spark.

In fact, as overblown and psuedotheological as American pulpit speech has become, any simple word is usually exciting. The obscure has now become the expected in the pulpit. Concrete speech is a solid contrast and a welcome relief from the vague fog that usually envelops the pulpit and pew.

Furthermore, the ideas of Lower Garble are ordinary. Not ordinary, like as in "understandable," but ordinary, like as in "trite." In fact, they are usually nothing but a string of religious clichés. The lower-garbling preacher may protest, "But I am no creative genius! What do they expect, anyhow?" It isn't genius that's lacking, however. It's usually work. Plain old ordinary, common work. Plus an attention to the Scripture, with its abundance of still-unheard ideas and yet-unthought thoughts.

The more the preacher depends upon his own creative topical efforts, the more ordinary his ideas become. The usual young preacher, fresh from the seminary, loaded (he thinks) with creative ideas, is usually in for a shock. He discovers that he only has three ideas anyway; and of these, everybody has heard two of them already, and the third isn't true. He has only two alternatives: trust in the Bible to provide ever-fresh, ever-meaningful ideas; or go on repeating his collection of inherited clichés.

Finally, the order of Lower Garble sermons is always predictable. First comes the text, then the introduction, then three points and a poem. Or first a problem, then a solution. The traditional preacher is predictably rigid; the avant-garde preacher, predictably amorphous. The evangelistic preacher is predictably authoritarian and hortatory; the counseling preacher, predictably nondirective. It becomes obvious that the form of the sermon is not the least bit influenced by the Scripture it generally claims to proclaim, but entirely by the life-style and theological bias of the preacher.

Again, the only cure for the predictable sameness of Lower Garble is for the preacher to take seriously both the real Word and the real world, and that will inevitably lead him to fresh-ness and discovery.

5. *Vaporizes each statement into a forceless mass.* Stylisti-cally, Lower Garble is hopeless. A dialect that is historically antique, uninvolved, talking with no imagination whatsoever to no one in particular about nothing in particular, could scarcely be expected to speak with impact. What causes its language to be so punchless?

(a) It avoids proper nouns and personal pronouns. This is the inevitable result of third-person preaching. Lower Garble iden-tifies no "us," no "we," no "you" or "I," only "it." This psuedo-objectivity loses not only personality, it loses the uniqueness of the present. Language struggles to express the unique. It cannot do so apart from the use of the *proper name,* which indicates without attempting definition or description. Casserly explains:

There is a sense in which all our words are shoddy and second-hand, used too often before, and by too many people, to be worthy of the exquisite individuality of the present event. . . . Let some modern Socrates ask John, an angelically patient John, why he loves Matilda. "Because of her brown eyes and auburn hair." "Because she is honest and kind and good." "But Ethel is all these things outstandingly." "Because she loves me." "But so does poor Joan." The conversation may continue till John's patience is exhausted, but it is certain that he will never succeed in telling his interrogator why he loves Matilda. If he is subtle enough John may say that he loves Matilda because of her "Matildaness"—in Christian theological and philosophical terms, the *hypostasis* or "hecceity" of Matilda—and this reply may terminate the conversation, but it will hardly answer the question. John has experienced "Matildaness" vividly enough, no doubt, but can he either describe or define it?[11]

Only preaching that names names, identifies places, and uses pronouns appropriately can hope to communicate personally and uniquely.

(b) It shuns actions verbs. Lower Garble depends upon the various forms of "to be," the weakest verb in the English language. For example, rather than saying, "He believes," Lower Garble prefers "It is his belief that." If it can avoid the verb altogether, so much the better: "Prior to the congregation's consideration of the suggestion," rather than, "Before the church considered the suggestion."

Whenever possible, Lower Garble adds to its general vagueness by using the more remote Latinate forms of verbs—"employ" instead of "use," "stated" instead of "said," "ensue" instead of "follow"—or else it changes them from verbs altogether: as "reflection" for "reflect," "consideration" for "considered," "investigation" for "investigate," and so on. Noun constructions and noun-adjectives replace vulgar verbs.

When they cannot be avoided, verbs can always be smothered by putting them in the passive voice. Inverting the sentence helps, too.

(c) It never uses simple adjectives or modifying phrases. For example, "psychological research" is too simple; "research of a psychological character" is much better. Putting adjectives after the nouns in prepositional phrases adds to the confusion: not, "it was a religious war," but "it was a war of a religious nature."

Categories should be added to all adjective complements: gigantic in size; triangular in shape; pure white in color. Otherwise, the listener might never figure this out for himself.

(d) It is wordy. Lower Garble never says one word when three would do just as well. It prefers "due to the reason that," not "because"; "in a manner similar to," not "like" or "as"; "in the event that," not "if." These phrases are not only longer, they are less precise. Lubricating phrases are dropped into the words to make the sentences slip along more smoothly: facilitate, effectuate, expedite, utilize; feasible, plausible, acceptable. The useless phrase, "the fact that," is constantly in use: "The fact that it rained hurt attendance"; not, "The rain hurt attendance."

The pulpit must overcome the dialect barriers of Upper Garble and Lower Garble to be heard. No doubt it can go on being a vaguely amusing and somehow comforting anachronism, a quaint remembrance of the good old days of virtue and innocence, of Sunday bandstands in the park and Fourth of July rhetoric, an occasionally pleasant pastoral interlude far from the "real world," the outside world. But if it does so, it can only expect amused tourists, not committed disciples.

Already thousands of the churches of the world have either become city monuments, brief stopovers for tour buses and curious visitors, or else obscure covens of the Society of the Same where only the dwindling number of initiates understand the strange dialect still doggedly spoken.

Not that the church should lose entirely the distinctiveness of its speech in a mere self-conscious effort to deny its heritage, in a silly attempt to "come home" to a world which is not its own; indeed, which is not even truly a *world,* but a *religion,* and a religion which is utterly foreign to its own faith. But it must break down the dialect walls which block its speech from reaching the world, the communication barriers which wall itself in and others out.

Dialect can only be eliminated by conversation. Only true conversation, conversation not with itself but with others, can overcome the regionalism of the pulpit. When conversation occurs, dialect disappears and understanding grows.

For the pulpit and pew, or for the preacher and layman, this interchange requires a peculiar grace, a unique humility. It requires a proper understanding of the diversity of gifts within the body of Christ, an acceptance of the function of the ministry and the importance of the laity. Both preacher and layman must stand beneath the Word; both must listen, and both must speak.

But how can the preacher so speak that he also hears, and is heard? And how can the layman so listen that he also speaks? There is a grace of hearing, and there is a gift of speaking. Unless preacher and congregation alike pray for both, no true dialogue can take place, and all of the external adjustment of its services or its speech cannot save it.

11

"THEY LISTENED
THE MORE WILLINGLY"

Delivery is not an art form; it is a communication channel.
Being a good speaker is not particularly important; being a
good communicator is. Of course, good communicators are
good speakers—but the opposite is not always true. What
usually happens when a preacher sets out to be a "good
speaker" is that he focuses on all the wrong things: eloquent
diction, precise enunciation, dramatic gestures, impressive
facial expression, resonant tone, even correct breathing. By the
time he is ready to speak, he is either paralyzed or galvanized.
On the platform he resembles either a chalk dummy or a zinc-
coated corpse.

An incarnational approach to sermon delivery is at least as
important as an incarnational approach to sermon theory.
When delivery is not fully integrated theologically into preaching, one of two things happens: Either it preoccupies itself with
the audience, which is the result of a false subjectivity; or it
preoccupies itself with its material, which is the result of a false
objectivity.

Subjectivity and Objectivity in Delivery

When delivery is treated as an art form to be mastered, a false
subjectivity arises. This preacher believes that his skill is
responsible for making the Word effective. Then we are treated

to the spectacle of the orating, gesticulating, posturing preacher. His delivery may be country-crude or city-slick, but he is still guilty of the same theological error: His attention is focused on himself and his effect rather than on the gospel and his congregation.

He may talk a great deal about the power of the Word or the authority of the Bible, but his every movement makes it apparent that his only trust is in himself, in his own ability to persuade or captivate. He has no confidence in the presence of God in his Word, or else he would trust himself to it more and less to his stage effects. If he really believed that the Bible possesses the power he is eternally asserting it has, he would not find it necessary to keep on blowing his trumpet so loudly or marching around the pulpit seven times in order to make the walls of Jericho fall down.

On the other hand, when delivery is treated homiletically as the illegitimate stepchild of the sermon, or as a mere afterthought, an interesting elective if one is so inclined, then another bad thing happens to preaching. Philosophically, it becomes Greek rather than Hebrew. The manuscript is the pure soul; delivery is the embarrassing body. Eventually only the soul is important, and the more disembodied it can remain, the better. Therefore the manuscript is usually read word for word—preferably in an unemotional monotone—to keep personality out of preaching as much as possible. (But then why not mimeograph the sermon and mail it to the congregation, thereby sparing them the boredom of hearing it badly read?)

There is a false objectivity at work here, as if the manuscript written by a very subjective human being is any less tainted with subjectivity than his speaking of it. But somehow the objectification of ideas on paper seems pure, whereas the delivery of these ideas orally introduces a corrupt and fallible subjectivity. The pure ideal, so coolly remote and mysteriously authoritative, has to undergo the humiliation of taking on shape and form with the attendant risk that someone will identify the preacher of it as a human being.

It is as if "Oz, the great and terrible" had to step out from behind his screen, where he is furiously cranking wheels and pulling levers, and show Dorothy that he is nothing more than a genial old man; or as when Alice screamed at the mad court, "You're nothing but a pack of cards!" and the whole thing tumbled together.

But poor delivery is no pure virtue, and saying a sermon badly is no evidence that God is in it. Monotone cannot prevent manipulation, and at least as many people have been deceived by false ideas as by false rhetoric.

Contact Point

Delivery must partake of the incarnational approach to preaching. Just as the interpretation of the Scripture must stand at midpoint between the historical and the existential, so delivery must stand at midpoint between the objective and the subjective, between a self-conscious withdrawal and an aggressive authoritarianism.

The *contact point* of the preached message is of utmost importance. The sermon must not take place behind the pulpit, nor on top of the pew, but at midpoint. True preaching only occurs when the preacher and his congregation meet halfway in dialogue.

This means that proper delivery neither attacks the congregation nor hides behind the pulpit. If the preacher is too aggressively outgoing, his audience may be impressed with the first few blasts of pure personality, but eventually they get tired of leaning backward to get his face out of theirs and move away from him. This kind of pulpit-pounding, Bible-twisting, Lord's Supper table-leaping preacher can stun the most faithful into a blank-faced, mindless withdrawal. But if the preacher himself is too withdrawn, too passive, the people may move toward him at first to encourage him to come out of hiding, but finally they will get tired of chasing him around the pulpit and decide the chase is not worth the effort. Let him burrow up in his notes; they have better things to do.

To establish the contact point of his sermon correctly, the preacher must maintain the proper linear distance relative to his material and his audience. This can only happen if he has the proper degree of confidence in both. If he is uncertain or insecure about his material or his audience, he will either get lost in his ideas or try to cover up his insecurity with a showy display of meaningless fireworks. But if he has too much self-assurance in his own brilliant ideas or his own magnetic personality, the same thing happens. He becomes so fascinated wih his own profound thoughts that he conducts a narcissistic love affair with them in plain sight of the audience, or else he trusts his own persuasive personality to the degree that he ignores the biblical message and depends upon dazzling the audience with his grand presence.

The preacher must believe in both the Word and his hearers. Then his delivery can be confident without being overconfident, natural without being forced, persuasive without being seductive. When he trusts God rather than himself, his confidence in his message is properly placed and his natural assurance grows. Likewise, when the preacher respects the integrity of his congregation, he does not attempt to overwhelm them or deceive them, but neither is he intimidated by them or afraid to share himself with them.

Sometimes the actual physical distance between the pulpit and the pew makes the proper contact point difficult to establish. But the mental stance of the preacher is far more important than his spatial location. *He should imagine himself standing at least one-third of the way down the rows of pews,* as much in the midst of the people as possible. This psychological stance is highly important. It prevents aloof, remote, abstract speech. It also makes it impossible to take on a false platform manner, or to shout or use grotesque gestures. (Only the most seriously imbalanced preacher could stand in the midst of his friends and orate, or shout in the face of someone only two feet away.)

This stance also permits the sermon to find its correct contact point. Since it neither hides from the audience nor overwhelms them, this kind of preaching encourages the people to meet the preacher halfway. They do not feel that the preacher is doing it all for them, and so they do not merely sit as passive spectators. Likewise, they do not feel that he has nothing to say, or that he is unsure of himself and unable to say anything with certainty, and so they do not feel that listening to him is a waste of time. Instead, the preacher preaches so that the sermon event takes place at midpoint, exactly halfway between the eagerness of the preacher to declare the message and the willingness of the congregation to hear it.

It is amazing what a transformation this simple mental positioning can cause in sermon delivery, in the naturalness and humanity it can bring to pulpit speech. And it is likewise amazing what it can do for the attentiveness of the congregation.

There is nothing like the sound of a familiar voice to catch attention. As Paul was being dragged toward the tower of Antonius (Acts 21), having just been rescued by the Roman guards from a Jewish mob who believed he had desecrated the temple, he asked the soldiers if he might speak to the crowd. They agreed; and when the people realized that he spoke their own language, they stopped their shouting, and "they listened the more willingly" (Acts 22:2).

If people ignore speech that is unnatural and peculiar, they are powerfully arrested by someone who speaks their own language. But "speaking their own language" involves more than voice or vocabulary, though of course these are involved. It is the complete impression conveyed from the pulpit. As such, it means that the preacher must talk about things that really matter to the people, that he must do so naturally and understandably, and that he must do this as one of them, not as an outsider. In short, he must practice conversational delivery. But what is that?

Conversational Delivery

Conversational delivery is no new concept. It is one of the most familiar phrases in homiletics. Some preachers enthusiastically believe in it and recommend it, while others just as soundly oppose it. But few terms are used more glibly and with less understanding of their meaning than "conversational preaching." What does it really mean? Or perhaps better, what *should* it mean?

The concept has a long history. It could be traced back to the ancient preachers who encouraged speech that the audience could understand, or even further, to the Greek orators who urged their pupils to use intimate, familiar speech. But apparently the primary origin of the modern concept dates back to Richard Baxter. In *The Reformed Pastor,* he wrote: "A great matter also with the most of our hearers doth lie in the very pronunciation and tone of speech. . . . Especially see that there be no affectation, but that we speak as familiarly to our people as we would if we were talking to any of them personally. The want of a familiar tone and expression is as great a defect in most of our deliveries as anything whatsoever, and that which we should be very careful to amend. When a man hath a reading or declaiming tone, like a schoolboy saying his lesson or an oration, few are moved with anything that he saith."[1]

Later preachers also took up this approach. It probably explains the appeal of Phillips Brooks better than anything else. A contemporary of his said, "He spoke to his audience *as a man might speak to his friend.* . . . The listeners never thought of style or manner, but only of the substance of his thoughts."[2] Charles R. Brown, dean of Yale Divinity School, said, "*The tone of dignified conversation* furnishes the staple method for effective delivery. It wears better than any other style of speech."[3] Harry Emerson Fosdick believed strongly in the conversational approach, but he never believed that he mastered it.[4] Helmut Thielicke stressed the importance of mastering one's sermon material in order to achieve conversational delivery: "Only he who is very familiar with and close to what he is saying can talk about it *quite naturally and in a conversational tone.*"[5]

Other preachers either strongly endorsing or known for practicing conversational delivery include John A. Broadus, who was a master of it, Charles Finney, John Henry Jowett, Dwight Moody, S. Parkes Cadman, Ralph Sockman, Clovis Chappell, and Leslie Weatherhead.

But what does conversational preaching involve? Before identifying some characteristics of the conversational style, let us first be plain about what it is *not*. It is not uninvolved, matter-of-fact, indifferent speech. It is not poorly articulated, overly quiet, mumbling speech. It is not inanimate, gestureless, expressionless speech. It is not a self-conscious monologue.

Conversational preaching, very simply, is exactly like a good conversation. Watch any two friends in conversation. Are they passive, expressionless? Or are they flamboyant and oratorical? Not if they are really having a conversation instead of holding alternating monologues. The amazing thing about conversation is that it can be so animated and lively without once appearing forced or unnatural. The whole business proceeds naturally.

This is the key to conversational preaching, and leads us to our first principle:

(1) *Conversational preaching is natural because it is internally motivated.* The preacher does not plan expressions, gestures, inflections. He allows these things to proceed naturally from the subject he is discussing. If he is fully involved with his subject, and at the same time completely engaged with his audience, the inevitable result will be a natural, animated style.

(2) *Conversational preaching speaks in its natural tone of voice.* Conversation is the speech norm. Everyone has a natural pitch of voice which he uses in daily conversation. That same tone should be carried to the platform. This does not mean that the voice may not need to be louder. Actually, the very physical difference between speaking to one person three feet away and five hundred people many feet away may demand more volume. But the secret is to use the same *tone*, even at a higher volume. This will require some practice at first, but it can be mastered if the preacher is really absorbed in genuine conversation. Do not elevate the pitch or fall into an oratorical cadence, the famous "ministerial tune." (This tune can actually be played on the piano: two notes the same, two notes one step higher, and then the first two notes repeated—try it sometime. On the piano—not the congregation!)

A voice pattern invariably results from a preset inflection which is unrelated to the content of the material being deliv-

ered. *This tone must be avoided at all costs.* Nothing so termi-
nates a conversation as the opening note of an oratorical solo,
and nothing so prevents a conversation from ever getting
started as the pious sing-song of Reverend Holier-Than-Thou.

(3) *Conversational preaching talks with its audience, not to
them, or at them.* It does so by including them in the thought
process. The preacher is not talking *to* the congregation about
his subject; he is talking *with* them about a mutual interest.
Talking *to* the audience suggests too strongly a one-sided
performance. He is certainly not talking *at* them either, as if
they were bad children who needed scolding, or even children
at all, who needed someone to tell them what to do.

Preaching is not telling someone what to do; it is a mutual
hearing of the word of God, as both speaker and listener stand
beneath its truth.

One useful means of achieving conversation with the audience is the rhetorical question. Flat assertions have a way of
shutting off discussion. (You can observe that in any daily
conversation.) As much as possible, the preacher should raise
questions to engage his congregation in mental dialogue: "How
can we love our neighbor? Isn't that really unrealistic and
impossible? And who is our neighbor, anyhow?" Or, "What do
you understand Christ to be saying in this Scripture? It seems
to me that he is asking. . . ." The sermon should be a mental
conversation: "I suppose it was something like that which
caused David to say. . . ." These sentences invite the congregation to join in the decision-making process.

(4) *Conversational preaching is constantly aware of the
audience.* Since the preacher is in conversation with his congregation, he is not oblivious to their response. He should
never be out of touch with their feelings, not even for a
moment. With practice, he should be able to detect instantly
the feelings his audience is constantly transmitting to him: If
his interpretation of the Scripture has struck a particularly
deep chord of response, he should know it; if boredom and
restlessness is spreading through the congregation, he should
know it. (One particularly accurate indication of not listening
is that blank look of solemn attention when the congregation is

sitting stone-still and motionless, as in a hypnotic trance—but if you waved a hand in front of their eyes, nobody would blink.)

The preacher must be so in control of his material that he can devote his full attention to conversation with his audience and reacting to their response. Chrysostom was so in touch with his congregation that he lengthened or shortened each section of his exposition depending upon the response of the audience.[6] Any preacher who has such a healthy respect for the reaction of his hearers will soon learn how to speak so that people listen willingly.

Understood in this way, conversational preaching is very closely akin to the dialogue sermon. It is not necessary to replace one with the other. The dialogue sermon is a special sermon *form,* and an excellent one, and depending upon the interest of the preacher and his congregation, may be used almost exclusively or very seldom.

But conversational preaching is a fundamental *approach* to the minister's role in the proclamation of the gospel. It can be used in every sermon, regardless of its form. It permits a distinct quality of dialogue even in traditional preaching where the minister alone speaks.

If the sermon does *not* engage the audience in mental dialogue, it is highly unlikely that actual physical dialogue can be structured after the sermon—or during it, for that matter, if the preacher is so flatly monological in his response or questioning that he squelches a scheduled dialogue session. After all, merely physically arranging a dialogue sermon is no guarantee that dialogue will actually take place. Who hasn't sat through a miserable session that advertised itself as a dialogue experience, but in fact was nothing but a series of alternating monologues?

Bonhoeffer insisted that dialogue could, and in fact, must occur in every true sermon:

What is the sociological relation of the congregation to the preacher? Is he drawn into their fellowship as one questioner among others? Or is he the bearer of unconditioned truth, and is he their teacher, answering their questions? Should the sermon be a dialogue or a monologue? . . . In answering this question . . . there has been a great deal of one-sided argument. It is characteristic of the preacher that he simultaneously questions and proclaims. He must ask along with the congregation, and form a "Socratic" community—otherwise he could not give any reply. But he can reply, and he must, because he knows God's answer in Christ. . . . It is a pre-supposition of a Christian congregation that it comes together as a questioner, and at the same time it is the strength of the congregation that each individual learns of the knowledge and the truth that belongs to the congregation.[7]

But this kind of dialogue through conversational preaching can be easily blocked. The preacher must avoid or remove those barriers that can block the communication channel.

Barriers in the Communication Channel

All of the barriers to true conversation have one thing in common: they are various forms of a *separation* between the speaker and the hearer. In order to participate in true dialogue with his congregation, the preacher must avoid each of these causes of separation:

(1) *Material separation.* When the preacher is preoccupied with his material, or else has not sufficiently mastered it, material separation occurs. He gets lost in his content and loses sight of the audience. This may be called "talking within the cylinder"; the preacher looks like a man in a phone booth reading the directory aloud to himself.

This fault has one of two causes. It will always occur if the preacher regards the sermon as a performance, as the delivery of a body of material, and so talks *about it* rather than *with the people.* But he can also be separated from the audience by his material if he must spend most of his time rummaging around in his mental attic trying to remember what in the world it was he wanted to say. Only adequate preparation and a proper focus can prevent this error. (Needless to say, anyone who obviously reads his sermon with his nose buried in a notebook hasn't got a chance to begin with. His material separation is absolute.)

(2) *Idea separation.* Idea separation is closely akin to material separation. But in this case it is not the material in general that causes the problem, but the presentation of abstract ideas. In other words, as long as the preacher is talking about personal events or is involved in narration, he is in close contact with his audience. His tone is natural, his manner friendly and relaxed. But let him begin to present a theory, a doctrine, or an abstract idea, and he lapses into impersonal oratory. His presentation sounds exactly like two different sermons delivered by two entirely different people.

This schizoid presentation can be avoided if the preacher realizes that all doctrines were given for people and that each of his ideas must be grasped by people. No part of the sermon should be thought of as theoretical; the most profound concepts have the most practical significance for people. Jesus always spoke most concretely and humanly when presenting his most eternal truths.

(3) *Mood separation.* Frequently the preacher begins on a higher level of emotional intensity than his audience. He has been thinking about his text and his sermon long enough—hopefully—that he has become genuinely excited about it and eager to communicate it. He may be tempted into a dramatic opening that strikes the audience as forced or unnatural simply because they do not as yet have any reason to be as fired about the subject as the preacher. Then when he realizes he has overshot his audience, he may panic at their lack of response and turn up the emotional level even higher in an attempt to whip the audience into enthusiasm. He may be guilty of *homiletical overkill:* emotion in excess of content, volume level in excess of space.

But rather than stirring emotion, just the opposite results. The congregation sits coldly watching a desperate performance, and he who has begun on a shout ends in a whisper.

Dynamism at the beginning of a sermon can be easily overdone. The preacher will do better to give the audience time and cause to be excited. He must realize that his own enthusiasm originated from the word of God and his study of it, and if properly presented it will do the same for the congregation. No hard and fast rule can be given in this area, but generally speaking an easy opening is an asset for gaining attention and a dynamic one a liability; whereas later in the sermon, dynamism may be appropriate and a casual stance less so.

It is also a mistake to begin to urge too soon in the sermon. In conversation, we never begin with exhorting. If we are ever led to urge or exhort a friend in conversation, such exhortation comes slowly and it is always marked by understanding, even humility. In order to be heard and heeded when we urge something upon a congregation of fellow Christians, we must first have demonstrated that we speak out of genuine interest in their well-being, that we profoundly care about them and understand them. Then our most serious words will be taken as the genuine concern of a real friend.

(4) *Pace separation.* Famous speakers have demonstrated a great variety in rate of delivery: Webster spoke at 80–100 words a minute; Lincoln, 100; Franklin Roosevelt, 117; Henry Clay, 160; and Phillips Brooks, 215 words a minute. Some people can obviously speak clearly and effectively at a much higher rate than others. But Brigance concludes, "In general a rate of more than 150 words a minute is too fast; and, if you slow down to 100 words a minute, there is danger of the audience losing interest—unless you speak with exceptional force and with effective pauses."[8]

Obviously it is possible to speak so rapidly that no one can follow, or so slowly that no one wants to follow. Static rate-figures, however, are not nearly so important as the *variety* of pace used by the speaker. Does his rate suit his subject matter? Is it internally motivated and natural, or artificial and forced? Does it ever vary, or is it uniformly hammering or uniformly dragging?

Floating is a pleasant sensation in water, but an extremely unpleasant one in preaching. The audience will invariably get restless and irritated if the preacher drifts aimlessly between thoughts, floating around and paddling along until he can think of something else to say. On the other hand, *racing* is equally irritating and nerve-racking. The preacher who leaps to the platform with his tongue racing is trying to pump into the sermon artificially the appearance of that conviction which it lacks naturally. Rate normally rises with enthusiasm or interest, but it should do so on its own, not as a device employed by the preacher to simulate fervor.

If a speaker is aware that his rate is naturally slow and deliberate, he can eliminate overly drawn-out pauses and add variety. Checking his energy level will be more productive than artificially increasing his rate; sometimes a too-slow rate is the result of an inadequate involvement with the sermon itself.

If he speaks too rapidly, the preacher can employ more pauses—the "white space" in oral delivery. Setting off sentences in print with "white space" separates them and emphasizes them. Pauses will do the same for the rapid speaker. He might also check his output of nervous energy. It could be that he lacks the certainty and assurance which God has promised to his servants.

Preaching and Conventional Speech Concerns

But what of the conventional concerns of "public speaking" classes—articulation, resonation, phonation, breathing, gestures, posture, and so on? Generally speaking, *these things are only important if they get in the way.* If communication is hindered by some fault in one of them, then the obstacle that is interfering must be removed from the communication channel. Enormous amounts of energy and time have been wasted by preachers and preaching classes in really pointless efforts to "master the arts" of gestures, articulation, breathing, and voice projection.

If the communication of the sermon is not being hampered by one of these elements, *no attention should be given to them whatsoever.* In fact positive harm can be done to the preacher and his proclamation by making him self-conscious about his speech. Then he focuses on the *externals* of the sermon rather than the *internal* matters from which good delivery proceeds. Even when a real problem is discovered, a point of diminishing returns is reached very quickly in efforts devoted to such "speech arts."

Artificiality can be easily created in the total delivery of a speaker who may suffer from poor articulation, for example, but who is otherwise completely natural and engaging. Instead of a very natural and earnest preacher of the gospel whose communication was really excellent except for rare occasions when faulty articulation blocked understanding, we are left with an overly precise and very self-conscious, artificial pulpit-orator who is anything but human and whose communication with his congregation is almost always bad. If that is improvement, the church doesn't need it.

The difficult problem for the preacher is knowing whether he has a speech problem that is interfering with the communication of his message, and if so, how to remove it. His college speech courses or seminary delivery courses should have at least indicated his problems. If not, then he must ask someone who knows him well enough to answer.

As for removing the problem, this first step is the hardest— suspecting that it is there, and asking. After that, the second step is conscious attention to eliminating the fault. This effort will have the undesirable, but inescapable, effect of making the preacher self-conscious for awhile. He will simply have to put up with that until the fault is gone. In the meantime, the best thing he can do is try to keep the rest of his delivery as natural as possible. The self-attention required to overcome a problem is a drastic cure, but if the fault is serious enough it may be warranted.

Finally, a few positive suggestions in each of these speech areas may be of some additional help.

1. *Body-language.* Almost nobody worries about gestures anymore, but body-language has become a topic of real interest. There are still many preachers who are either grotesque or frozen in the pulpit. The total absence of bodily involvement is as much a distraction to an audience as constant arm-waving or

repetitious finger-stabbing. The use of the body, like all of delivery, must be internally motivated. Everyone uses gestures naturally in conversation because they are only done spontaneously; but put the same natural conversation-gesturer on the platform, and he may freeze or flap. He won't, if he is really set free through genuine conversation with his audience.

Body language, then, can never be planned. It happens. How can a natural use of the body be encouraged?

(a) *By not studying gestures.* Nothing is more fatal than practicing in front of a mirror, or studying "upper, middle, and lower plane" gestures. That kind of planning is a sure-fire way to artificiality. Whoever thought of planning a gesture for conversation? "Let's see—this afternoon when I tell Tom about my flight from New York, I think I'll point heavenward!"

(b) *By not preventing body involvement.* Body involvement is only totally absent if prevented. If we mask our faces to hide our feelings, or stand woodenly to avoid making a mistake, we make a mistake. Sometimes the problem lies in the feeling-level of the preacher, too. If we are indifferent, we rarely gesture. The only body movements that should be prevented are meaningless, grotesque, or repetitious gestures which may be habitual but are never natural.

(c) *By avoiding overkill.* Homiletical overkill—emotion in excess of content, volume level in excess of space—always results in exaggerated, artificial expressions and movements. Forcing emotion forces gestures, often wildly inappropriate and poorly timed. But funny.

(d) *By becoming involved with the issue.* Involvement with the subject-matter of the sermon leads to spontaneous, appropriate body movement—just as it does in conversation.

(e) *By becoming involved with the audience.* Body language is often produced in conversation because of our relationship with our listener: We smile or frown because of the feelings we share with him; we point toward him, or left or right of him; we stretch our hands to measure for him; we shrug to indicate a feeling we can't verbalize to him.

(f) *By becoming involved with the pictures.* When we are

really visualizing our subject, or when we are absorbed in narration, we use our bodies unselfconsciously. These are usually totally spontaneous expressions of the most appropriate sort. The more we visualize our ideas, the more visible they become to the audience.

(g) *By stretching yourself.* A few preachers are too big for any platform, but many are too small. They simply feel awkward holding a lively conversation with more than one person. Often they feel that they are overly gesturing and that their facial expressions are already almost too much. Usually the opposite is true. Just as a larger room requires more volume, a larger conversation can stand broader movement without becoming unnatural.

One good exercise for the really inhibited preacher is telling made-up stories to children. Expressiveness and natural body use always result from this kind of fun. And if you don't have any children of your own to tell stories to, rent some!

2. *Articulation, resonation, phonation.* Each of these terms has to do with speech sounds. *Phonation* is simply producing sound. *Articulation* is shaping it. *Resonation* is amplifying it.

The sound produced by the vibration of the vocal folds has a definite pitch, largely determined by the length and thickness of those folds. Most people produce adequate sound for speech. Endless amounts of needless effort have been devoted by preachers to developing a "deeper" voice. For their trouble, they are usually rewarded only with a monotone. The sole requirement for a good voice is that it be interesting. Variety in tone accomplishes that. And variety results from internally motivated speech. Virtually the only time that a voice needs to be lowered is when it is artificially elevated by tension.

Nothing is worse for Christian proclamation than for a preacher to become enamored with his own sounds. But he should be alert for persistent hoarseness, which may indicate constant voice abuse through harsh, strident misuse, but which can also be a symptom of serious throat problems. A doctor should always be consulted immediately if hoarseness persists longer than two weeks.

Resonation, or the amplification of the voice, is largely accomplished in the upper resonating chambers behind the nose, although the mouth plays- some part. If the preacher's voice lacks adequate resonation, or the famous "voice projection," all he usually needs to do is open his mouth. Proper tone placement is impossible with teeth clenched. Nasality is also prevented in the same way. If either of these is a problem, a good exercise is to speak with the front teeth at least one-half inch apart: practice speaking with a notched eraser, cut to the proper length, held between the front teeth. (This is about as odd as speech exercises get, but it will correct severe nasality or inadequate voice projection.)

Articulation has to do with the cleanness and distinctness with which words are shaped. As long as all of the sounds in a word are easily understandable, articulation is adequate. Overly precise articulation, or the strange pronunciation of the speech purist who insists on saying all of the letters in a word—even those that shouldn't be pronounced, such as the "i" in glacier or marriage—sounds prissy and pedantic.

But if some words are not coming across clearly to the audience because of slurred vowels or dropped consonants, then articulation needs attention. The problem is usually either regional speech faults (dropping final g's, as in "runnin'"; or dark vowels, such as "dork" for "dark"), or that the preacher is lip-lazy. More active, precise use of the lips and tongue in clipping off sounds will correct the problem.

3. *Breathing.* Unless the preacher is gasping like a guppy, or running out of air in the middle of sentences, no attention needs to be given to breathing. Only the miracles of Lourdes are a more fascinating mystery than the fabled diaphramatic breathing. It would be interesting to know how many hours have been spent by preachers standing around with their hands on their middles, panting like puppy-dogs; or how many sermons have been delivered in an absent-minded way by preachers lost in the mysterious contemplation of "packing their tones around their belt"—whatever that means.

If the speaker will simply not preach at such a ridiculous rate that he sounds like a man simultaneously running to a fire and delivering the Gettysburg address; or if he does not studiously cultivate that curious gasping sound before every sentence which is supposed to simulate religious passion; or if he will not speak out of half-exhausted lungs, sipping teaspoonsful of air between words; then he need not worry about mastering the mysteries of diaphramatic breathing or avoiding the curse of "upper-clavicular breathing" (which, to everyone's pleasure, will remain undefined).

4. *Posture and platform manner.* The last of the classical speech concerns to be discussed here are posture and platform manner, which require the least comment of all. Unless a preacher is either rigid with fright or is possessed with a length of rubber hose for a backbone, posture is insignificant. Common sense should take care of platform manner. A few "don'ts" should suffice:

(a) Don't bound to the platform like an escaped kangaroo, nor drag to the platform like a man going to the block.

(b) Don't slump across the pulpit as if unable to remain awake (others may join you).

(c) Don't stand ram-rod stiff and rigid, as though afraid of setting off a bomb.

(d) Don't fix your gaze on the ceiling, the floor, or one side of your audience alone. (Eye-contact in conversation is natural; it doesn't need promoting, just not preventing.)

(e) Don't rock back and forth or sway hypnotically from side to side like a cobra about to strike. (This is a hard habit to break, if habitual. Try anchoring one leg against the back of the pulpit. That is a frightful unnatural stance, but it is much less distracting than the preacher who has got into a "weaving way." In time, it can be easily abandoned.)

In summary, delivery should be natural. It will be, if internally motivated. Conversation is its model because it is the basic speech norm. It is a style of speech exactly suited to the Christian message. Conversational preaching avoids both false subjectivity and false objectivity and permits the most intimate communication of the word of God to men.

Approached in this way, the delivery of the sermon stands miles apart from the Emerson School of Elocution tradition, the self-conscious mastery of an impressive art-form. Sermon delivery must be anchored on its subjective side to communication theory, and on its objective side to incarnational preaching. Otherwise it will falsify its theological basis at the same time it is failing to communicate.

But when the living Word becomes incarnate in the living situation—even as it takes on flesh and blood in the most practical saying of the sermon—then the preaching event occurs, and Christ once again comes to his people.

NOTES

Preface

1. Julius Schniewind, *Die geistliche Erneuerung des Pfarrerstandes,* 2nd ed. (Berlin: Verlag Haus und Schule, 1949), p. 7.

2. Gustaf Wingren, *The Living Word* (Philadelphia: Fortress Press, 1960), p. 24.

3. Ibid., pp. 23–24.

4. Joseph Sittler, *The Anguish of Preaching* (Philadelphia: Fortress Press, 1966), p. 7.

5. Ibid., p. 10.

6. Ibid., p. 12.

7. Rudolf Bohren, *Preaching and Community,* trans. David E. Green (Richmond: John Knox Press, 1965), p. 42.

8. David James Randolph, *The Renewal of Preaching* (Philadelphia: Fortress Press, 1969), p. 21. We cannot agree with David Randolph at this point when he places the ax in the hands of venerable John A. Broadus, who may have compounded the crime but certainly was not responsible for it. That atrocity was committed long before Broadus asserted that homiletics was a branch of rhetoric.

1. The Stubborn Pulpit

1. Fred B. Craddock, *As One without Authority* (Enid, Okla.: Phillips University Press, 1971), p. 1.

2. T. Harwood Pattison, *The History of Christian Preaching* (Philadelphia: American Baptist Publication Society, 1903), p. 88.

3. Yngve Brilioth, *A Brief History of Preaching*, trans. Karl E. Mattson (Philadelphia: Fortress Press, 1965), pp. 21 ff.

4. Pattison, *History of Christian Preaching*, p. 57.

5. Brilioth, *Brief History of Preaching*, p. 95.

6. Ibid., pp. 79–81.

7. Clyde E. Fant, Jr. and William M. Pinson, Jr., *20 Centuries of Great Preaching*, 13 vols. (Waco, Tex.: Word Books, 1971), 1:232.

8. Ibid.

9. Brilioth, *Brief History of Preaching*, pp. 129 ff.

10. Pattison, *History of Christian Preaching*, p. 211.

11. Richard Baxter, *The Reformed Pastor*, ed. Hugh Martin (Richmond: John Knox Press, 1956), p. 89.

12. Pattison, *History of Christian Preaching*, p. 248.

13. Stopford Brooke, ed., *Life and Letters of Frederick W. Robertson*, 2 vols. (Boston: Ticknor and Fields, 1865), 2:59–60.

14. Ibid.

15. Joseph Fort Newton, *Some Living Masters of the Pulpit* (New York: George H. Doran Co., 1923), pp. vii–viii.

16. *Spectator*, 91:85–86.

17. *Current Literature*, 42: 312–14.

18. Ibid., 44:94–95.

19. *Harper's Weekly*, 55:6.

20. *Hampton's Magazine*, 27:223–32.

21. *Current Opinion*, 69:511–12.

22. *Literary Digest*, 83:34.

23. *Literary Digest*, 87:31–32.

24. *Century Magazine*, 111:1–18.

25. *Harper's Magazine*, 157:133–41.

26. *Christian Century*, 49:114–16.

27. *Catholic World*, 144:6–8.

28. Joseph Sittler, *The Anguish of Preaching* (Philadelphia: Fortress Press, 1966), p. 26.

29. Clyde Reid, *The Empty Pulpit* (New York: Harper & Row, 1967), pp. 25–33.

30. Reuel Howe, *Partners in Preaching* (New York: Seabury Press, 1967), pp. 26–33.

31. Gene E. Bartlett, "The Preaching and Pastoral Roles," *Pastoral Psychology* 3 (March 1952): 21–28.

32. Pierre Berton, *The Comfortable Pew* (New York: J. B. Lippincott & Co., 1965), pp. 96 ff.

33. Peter Berger, *The Noise of Solemn Assemblies* (Garden City, N.Y.: Doubleday, 1961).

34. Rodney Stark et al., "Sounds of Silence," *Psychology Today* 3, no. 11 (April 1970): 38 ff.

35. James E. Dittes, *Minister on the Spot* (Philadelphia: Pilgrim Press, 1970), pp. 77–78.

36. Reuel Howe, *The Miracle of Dialogue* (New York: Seabury Press, 1963), p. 32.

37. Berton, *The Comfortable Pew*, pp. 101–2.

38. Horst Symanowski, *The Christian Witness in an Industrial Society* (Philadelphia: Westminster Press, 1964), p. 20.

39. August Wenzel, "Criticisms of Preaching in Current Writings," *Lutheran Quarterly* 20 (November 1968): 393.

40. Theodore Wedel, "Is Preaching Outmoded?" *Religion in Life* 35 (Autumn 1965): 535.

41. Harvey Cox, *The Secular City* (New York: Macmillan Co., 1965), p. 122.

42. Helmut Thielicke, *The Trouble with the Church*, trans. & ed. John W. Doberstein (New York: Harper & Row, 1965), p. xi.

43. Robert Jensen, *A Religion Against Itself* (Richmond: John Knox Press, 1967).

44. Gerhard Ebeling, *Theology and Proclamation*, trans. John Riches (Philadelphia: Fortress Press, 1966).

45. Thielicke, *Trouble with the Church*, cf. pp. 9 ff.

46. Sittler, *Anguish of Preaching*, p. 27.

2. The Stubborn Hope

1. Amos N. Wilder, *The Language of the Gospel* (New York: Harper & Row, 1964), pp. 18–19.

2. Ibid., p. 14.

3. Ibid., p. 15.

4. Robert H. Mounce, *The Essential Nature of New Testament Preaching* (Grand Rapids: William B. Eerdmans Pub. Co., 1960), pp. 16–18.

5. Yngve Brilioth, *A Brief History of Preaching* (Philadelphia: Fortress Press, 1965), p. 3.

6. W. B. Sedgwick, "The Origins of the Sermon," *Hibbert Journal* 45 (January 1947): 162.

7. Yngve Brilioth, *Landmarks in the History of Preaching* (London: S.P.C.K., 1950), pp. 2–3.

8. Floyd V. Filson, *The New Testament Against Its Environment* (Chicago: Henry Regnery Co., 1950), p. 11.

9. P. T. Forsyth, *Positive Preaching and the Modern Mind* (Grand Rapids: Wm. B. Eerdmans Pub. Co., 1964), p. 1.

10. Filson, *New Testament Environment*, p. 26.

11. Thorleif Boman, *Hebrew Thought Compared with Greek* (Philadelphia: Westminster Press, 1960), p. 206.

12. P. H. Menoud, "Preaching," *The Interpreter's Dictionary of the Bible*, 4 vols. (Nashville: Abingdon Press, 1962), 3:868.

13. Jerome Murphy-O'Connor, *Paul on Preaching* (New York: Sheed & Ward, 1964), p. 51.

14. Wilder, *Language of the Gospel*, p. 28.

15. Ibid., p. 21.

16. Mounce, *New Testament Preaching*, p. 28.

17. Wilder, *Language of the Gospel*, p. 21.

18. Ibid., pp. 22–23.

19. Hugh Kerr, *Preaching in the Early Church* (New York: Fleming H. Revell Co., 1948), p. 14.

20. Wilder, *Language of the Gospel*, p. 20.

21. Clemens E. Benda, "Language, Consciousness and Problems of Existential Analysis (Daseinsanalyse)," *American Journal of Psychotherapy* 14, no. 2 (April 1960): 262.

22. Robert W. Funk, *Language, Hermeneutic, and Word of God* (New York: Harper & Row, 1966), p. 7.

23. Karl Barth, *The Preaching of the Gospel*, trans. B. E. Hooke (Philadelphia: Westminster Press, 1963), p. 9.

24. Ibid., pp. 12, 14.

25. Ibid., pp. 54–55.

26. Ibid., p. 37.

27. Carl E. Braaten, "The Interdependence of Theology and Preaching," *Dialog*, Winter 1964, p. 15.

28. Fred B. Craddock, *As One without Authority* (Enid, Okla.: Phillips University Press, 1971), p. 39.

29. Rudolf Bultmann, *Theologie des Neuen Testaments*, 3 vols. (Tübingen: J.C.B. Mohr, 1948), 1:297.

30. Rudolf Bultmann, "Reply," *The Theology of Rudolf Bultmann*, ed. Charles W. Kegley (New York: Harper & Row, 1966), pp. 260–61.

31. Ibid., p. 273.

32. Rudolf Bultmann, "Preaching: Genuine and Secularized," *Religion and Culture, Essays in Honor of Paul Tillich*, ed. Walter Leibrecht (New York: Harper & Brothers, 1959), p. 240.

33. Rudolf Bultmann, *Offenbarung und Heilsgeschehen*, vol. 7 of *Beitrage zur evangelischen Theologie*, ed. E. Wolfe (Munich: Evangelischer Verlag, Albert Lempp, 1941), 7:66.

34. For further documentation of this assertion, see my work, *Bonhoeffer: Worldly Preaching* (Nashville: Thomas Nelson and Sons, 1975).

35. Dietrich Bonhoeffer, *Gesammelte Schriften*, ed. Eberhard Bethge, 5 vols. (Munich: Chr. Kaiser Verlag, 1961), 4:7.

36. Ibid., 4:8.

37. Ibid., 4:12.

38. Ibid., 4:240.

39. Gerhard Ebeling, *The Problem of Historicity in the Church and Its Proclamation*, trans. Grover Foley (Philadelphia: Fortress Press, 1967), p. 22.

40. Gerhard Ebeling, *Word and Faith*, trans. James Leitch (Philadelphia: Fortress Press, 1963), p. 425.

41. Heinrich Ott, *Theology and Preaching*, trans. Harold Knight (Philadelphia: Westminster Press, 1965), p. 19.

42. Heinz Zahrnt, *The Question of God: Protestant Theology in the Twentieth Century*, trans. R. A. Wilson (New York: Harcourt, Brace & World, 1969), p. 299.

43. Gustaf Wingren, *The Living Word* (Philadelphia: Fortress Press, 1960), p. 13.

44. P. T. Forsyth, *Positive Preaching and the Modern Mind* (Grand Rapids: Wm. B. Eerdmans Pub. Co., 1964), p. 1.

45. Emil Brunner, *Revelation and Reason* (Philadelphia: Westminster Press, 1946), p. 142.

46. H. H. Farmer, *The Servant of the Word* (New York: Charles Scribner's Sons, 1942), p. 24.

47. Martin E. Marty, *Second Chance for American Protestants* (New York: Harper & Row, 1963), pp. 158–59.

48. Harvey Cox, *The Secular City* (New York: Macmillan Co., 1965), p. 241.

49. John Bright, *The Authority of the Old Testament* (Nashville: Abingdon Press, 1967), pp. 162, 164.

50. Nels F. S. Ferré, "The Place of Preaching in the Modern World," *The Pulpit*, December 1962, p. 10.

51. Clyde Reid, *The Empty Pulpit* (New York: Harper & Row, 1967), pp. 37–38.

52. Joseph Sittler, *The Anguish of Preaching* (Philadelphia: Fortress Press, 1966), pp. 7–8.

53. Peter L. Berger, "A Call for Authority in the Christian Community," unpublished manuscript (mimeo COCU: 71, Denver No. 9), pp. 9 ff.

54. Peter L. Berger, *The Precarious Vision* (Garden City, N.Y.: Doubleday and Co., 1961), p. 184.

55. Reid, *Empty Pulpit*, p. 86.

56. Gerhard Ebeling, *The Nature of Faith*, trans. Ronald Gregor Smith (Philadelphia: Muhlenberg Press, 1961), p. 189.

57. Ibid., p. 190.

3. Toward Incarnational Preaching

1. Peter L. Berger, "A Call for Authority in the Christian Community," unpublished manuscript (mimeo COCU: 71, Denver No. 9), pp. 6, 11.

2. Jürgen Moltmann, *Theology of Hope* (New York: Harper & Row, 1965), pp. 172–73.

3. Jules Moreau, *Language and Religious Language* (Philadelphia: Westminster Press, 1961), p. 194.

4. H. Richard Niebuhr, *Christ and Culture* (New York: Harper & Row, 1951), p. 11.

5. For his discussion of this subject, see *The Living Word* (Philadelphia: Fortress Press, 1960), pp. 25 ff.

6. Gustaf Wingren, *The Living Word* (Philadelphia: Fortress Press, 1960), p. 26.

7. Paul Tillich, *Theology of Culture* (New York: Oxford University Press, 1959), p. 204.

8. Ibid., p. 207.

9. Ibid., pp. 207, 208.

10. Wingren, *Living Word*, p. 211.

11. Tillich, *Theology of Culture*, p. 42.

12. Harvey Cox, *The Secular City* (New York: Macmillan Co., 1965), p. 241.

13. Emil Brunner, *The Divine-Human Encounter* (Philadelphia: Westminster Press, 1943), p. 85.

14. H. H. Farmer, *The Servant of the Word* (New York: Charles Scribner's Sons, 1942), p. 45.

15. Kyle Haselden, *The Urgency of Preaching* (New York: Harper & Row, 1963), p. 24.

16. Eberhard Bethge, *Bonhoeffer in a World Come of Age,* ed. Peter Vorkink II (Philadelphia: Fortress Press, 1968), p. 50. But it is interest-

ing to see his remark on the next page, "repetition has emptied the words" of preaching, which is certainly a criticism of its method of communication of the message.

17. Ronald E. Sleeth, "Theology vs. Communication Theories," *Religion in Life* 32 (Autumn 1963): 547–52.

18. Tillich, *Theology of Culture*, p. 201.

19. Ibid., p. 213.

4. *"We Are Men Like Yourselves"*

1. Helmut Thielicke, *The Trouble with the Church*, trans. and ed. John W. Doberstein (New York: Harper & Row, 1965), pp. 9–10.

2. George Buttrick, *Jesus Came Preaching* (New York: Charles Scribner's Sons, 1932), p. 170.

3. Charles H. Spurgeon, *Spurgeon's Lectures to His Students*, ed. David Otis Fuller (Grand Rapids: Zondervan Pub. House, 1945), p. 147.

4. P. T. Forsyth, *Positive Preaching and the Modern Mind* (Grand Rapids: Wm. B. Eerdmans Pub. Co., 1964), p. 41.

5. Dietrich Bonhoeffer, *Life Together*, trans. and intro. John W. Doberstein (New York: Harper & Bros., 1954), p. 108.

6. Dietrich Bonhoeffer, *Gesammelte Schriften*, ed. Eberhard Bethge, 5 vols. (Munich: Chr. Kaiser Verlag, 1961), 4:282.

7. Jaroslav Pelikan, *The Preaching of Chrysostom* (Philadelphia: Fortress Press, 1967), p. 24.

8. John Octavius Johnston, *The Life and Letters of Henry Parry Liddon* (New York: Longmans, Green & Co., 1904), p. 55.

9. D. T. Niles, *Preaching the Gospel of the Resurrection* (Philadelphia: Westminster Press, 1953), p. 45.

10. Karl Barth, *The Word of God and the Word of Man*, trans. Douglas Horton (New York: Harper & Bros., 1957), p. 129.

11. Paul Scherer, *For We Have This Treasure* (New York: Harper & Bros., 1944), p. 23.

12. Brand Blanshard, *On Philosophical Style* (Bloomington: Indiana University Press, 1954), p. 18.

13. John Kelman, *The War and Preaching* (New Haven: Yale University Press, 1919), pp. 9–10.

14. Clyde E. Fant, Jr., and William M. Pinson, Jr., *20 Centuries of Great Preaching*, 13 vols. (Waco, Tex.: Word Books, 1971), 5:51.

15. Blanshard, *Philosophical Style*, pp. 52–53.

5. Credibility and Charisma

1. This material follows the approach of Hovland, Janis, and Kelley in *Communication and Persuasion* (New Haven: Yale University Press, 1966), pp. 19–53. Other approaches of interest, with only slight variations, are given by C. H. Marple in the *Journal of Social Psychology* 4 (1933): 176–86 and Erwin Bettinghaus, *Persuasive Communication* (New York: Holt, Rinehart, & Winston, 1968), pp. 105 ff.

2. J. Edgar Park, *The Miracle of Preaching* (New York: Macmillan Co., 1936), p. 148.

3. See Clyde E. Fant, Jr., and William M. Pinson, Jr., *20 Centuries of Great Preaching*, 13 vols. (Waco, Tex.: Word Books, 1971), volumes 4 and 6.

4. Phillips Brooks, *Lectures on Preaching* (New York: E. P. Dutton & Co., 1898), p. 5.

5. Nathaniel J. Burton, *In Pulpit and Parish* (New York: Macmillan Co., 1925), p. 96.

6. Helmut Thielicke, *The Trouble with the Church*, trans. and ed. John W. Doberstein (New York: Harper & Row, 1965), pp. 23–24.

7. Ann Ruth Willner, *Charismatic Political Leadership: A Theory* (Princeton, N.J.: Center of International Studies, 1968), p. 16.

8. Erwin Bettinghaus, *Persuasive Communication* (New York: Holt, Rinehart & Winston, 1968), p. 117.

9. Willner, *Charismatic Political Leadership*, p. 4.

10. Ibid., p. 9.

11. Ibid., pp. 61 ff.

12. Ibid., p. 9.

7. The Word Becomes Flesh

1. Karl Barth, *The Preaching of the Gospel*, trans. B. E. Hooke (Philadelphia: Westminster Press, 1963), p. 77.

2. Ibid., p. 18.

3. Harry Emerson Fosdick, *The Living of These Days* (New York: Harper & Bros., 1956), pp. 95, 98.

4. Charles H. Spurgeon, *Spurgeon's Lectures to His Students*, ed. David Otis Fuller (Grand Rapids: Zondervan Pub. House, 1945), p. 66.

5. Heinrich Ott, *Theology and Preaching*, trans. Harold Knight (Philadelphia: Westminster Press, 1965), p. 68.

6. Edmund Holt Linn, *Preaching as Counseling: The Unique*

Method of Harry Emerson Fosdick (Valley Forge, Pa.: Judson Press, 1966), p. 55.

7. Paul Tillich, *Theology of Culture*, ed. Robert C. Kimbell (New York: Oxford University Press, 1959), p. 74.

8. John Killinger, ed., *Experimental Preaching* (New York: Abingdon Press, 1973), p. 15.

9. Rudolf Bultmann, *Jesus Christ and Mythology* (New York: Charles Scribner's Sons, 1958), pp. 41, 42.

10. Killinger, *Experimental Preaching*, p. 14.

11. Ibid., p. 13.

12. Ibid.

13. Ibid., pp. 9, 10.

8. Out of the Gutenberg Galaxy

1. Howard H. Martin, "Puritan Preachers on Preaching: Notes on American Colonial Rhetoric," *Quarterly Journal of Speech* 50, no. 3 (October 1964): 285.

2. For a discussion of the differences between oral and written style, see William Norwood Brigance, *Speech Composition* (New York: Appleton-Century Crofts, 1953), pp. 200 ff.; Raymond F. Howes, "The Talked and the Written," *Quarterly Journal of Speech* 26 (April 1940): 231 ff.; C. H. Woolberton, "Speaking and Writing—A Study of Differences," *Quarterly Journal of Speech Education*, June 1922, pp. 272 ff.; Glenn A. Capp, *How to Communicate Orally* (Englewood Cliffs, N.J.: Prentice-Hall, 1961), pp. 212 ff.

3. Marshall McLuhan and Edmund Carpenter, eds., *Explorations in Communication* (Boston: Beacon Press, 1960), pp. 125–26.

4. Marshall McLuhan, *The Gutenberg Galaxy, the Making of a Typographic Man* (Toronto: University of Toronto Press, 1962), p. 20.

5. Marshall McLuhan, *Understanding Media, the Extensions of Man* (New York: McGraw-Hill Book Co., 1964), p. 79.

6. McLuhan, *Gutenberg Galaxy*, p. 23.

7. Ibid., p. 98.

8. For a complete discussion of this question, see "A Study of the Effects of Certain Elements of Oral Style on the Intelligibility of Informative Speeches," unpublished dissertation by Gordon L. Thomas, Northwestern University, June 1952.

9. Karl Barth, *The Preaching of the Gospel*, trans. B. E. Hooke (Philadelphia: Westminster Press, 1963), p. 77.

10. "Some Said It Thundered":
Upper Garble and Lower Garble

1. Jacques Barzun, *House of Intellect* (New York: Harper & Bros., 1959), p. 222.

2. Jerome Herbert Perlmutter, *A Practical Guide to Effective Writing* (New York: Random House, 1965), p. 9.

3. Charles H. Spurgeon, *Spurgeon's Lectures to His Students*, ed. David Otis Fuller (Grand Rapids: Zondervan Pub. House, 1945), p. 200.

4. Austin Phelps, *English Style in Public Discourse* (New York: Charles Scribner's Sons, 1883), p. 341.

5. Helmut Thielicke, *The Trouble with the Church*, trans. and ed. John W. Doberstein (New York: Harper & Row, 1965), p. 54.

6. Harry Emerson Fosdick, *The Living of These Days* (New York: Harper & Bros., 1956), p. 92.

7. Dietrich Bonhoeffer, *Gesammelte Schriften*, ed. Eberhard Bethge, 5 vols. (Munich: Chr. Kaiser Verlag, 1961), 4:260.

8. Charles R. Brown, *The Art of Preaching* (New York: Macmillan Co., 1922), p. 42.

9. Fosdick, *Living of These Days*, p. 93.

10. Thielicke, *The Trouble with the Church*, p. 58.

11. Julian Victor Langmead Casserley, *The Christian in Philosophy* (New York: Charles Scribner's Sons, 1951), pp. 178–79.

11. "They Listened
the More Willingly"

1. Richard Baxter, *The Reformed Pastor*, ed. Hugh Martin, (Richmond: John Knox Press, 1956), pp. 97 ff.

2. Alexander V. G. Allen, *The Life and Letters of Phillips Brooks*, 3 vols. (New York: E. P. Dutton & Co., 1901), 3:393.

3. Charles R. Brown, *The Art of Preaching* (New York: Macmillan Co., 1922), p. 168.

4. See Clyde E. Fant, Jr., and William M. Pinson, Jr., *20 Centuries of Great Preaching*, 13 vols. (Waco, Tex.: Word Books, 1971), 9:24–25.

5. Helmut Thielicke, *Encounter with Spurgeon* (Philadelphia: Fortress Press, 1963), p. 32.

6. See Fant and Pinson, *20 Centuries,* 1:58 ff.

7. Dietrich Bonhoeffer, *The Communion of Saints,* trans. R. Gregor Smith (New York: Harper & Row, 1963), p. 165.

8. William Norwood Brigance, *Speech Communication* (New York: Appleton-Century Crofts, 1947), p. 58.